Distr.
GENERAL
E/ESCWA/SDPD/2005/9
24 October 2005
ORIGINAL: ENGLISH

ECONOMIC AND SOCIAL COMMISSION FOR WESTERN ASIA

UNIVERSITÉ D'OTTAWA
RÉSEAU DE BIBLIOTHÈQUE

MAY
MAI 2 4 2006

UNIVERSITY OF OTTAWA
LIBRARY NETWORK

DÉPÔT
DEPOSIT

ESCWA WATER DEVELOPMENT REPORT 1

VULNERABILITY OF THE REGION TO SOCIO-ECONOMIC DROUGHT

United Nations
New York, 2005

References have, wherever possible, been verified.

E/ESCWA/SDPD/2005/9
ISSN 1817-1990
ISBN 92-1-128294-2
05-0539

UNITED NATIONS PUBLICATION
Sales No. E.05.II.L.17

Executive summary

Of all natural hazards, drought affects the greatest number of people globally, with devastating impact. The vulnerability of communities to drought is dependent on a host of physical, social, environmental and economic characteristics. In recent years, owing to population growth, soil degradation, increased desertification, and projected climate change scenarios, drought research and planning has become crucial to averting and mitigating drought disasters. Drought vulnerability research examines how the impacts of drought are a result of the interactions of social, political and economic systems, as well as the meteorological drought phenomenon. However, in the past, drought monitoring and research focused almost exclusively on the relation of climatic patterns and rainfall deficiencies to water supply. However, such a focus does not examine how human water use exacerbates deficits in water supply and quality. As a result, there is a worldwide insufficiency of disaster preparedness and mitigation methods that adequately address the socio-economic effects of drought and integrate drought planning into water resource management.

The objective of the present study is to address the gap in understanding socio-economic drought in the Economic and Social Commission for Western Asia (ESCWA) region, and to raise awareness of the importance of developing drought detection, prevention, preparedness and mitigation measures regionally. In order to examine the socio-economic impacts of drought, this report presents measures taken on drought management and mitigation from three regional case-studies—Jordan, the Syrian Arab Republic and Yemen—and addresses the need for regional drought preparedness planning.

The ESCWA region. The ESCWA region is the most water-scarce region in the world, accounting for almost 5 per cent of the world's population, but less than 1 per cent of the world's freshwater resources. Rapid population and economic growth coupled with finite water resources have greatly reduced annual per capita freshwater resources, from 3,300 (cubic metres) m^3 in 1960 to 981 m^3 in 2000. The countries in this region live on per capita water consumption levels under or near the water poverty level of 1,000 m^3 per person per year.

The vulnerability of ESCWA member countries to drought has intensified owing to the region's demographic and economic growth, increasing water scarcity and water-resource and land-use patterns. Poor land-use practices, such as overgrazing, over-cultivation, and poor irrigation, have degraded and changed land characteristics, which have, in turn, changed the general climate in the region. The result is reduced rainfall and environmental degradation, which leads to desertification and increases drought vulnerability. In addition, over-exploitation and water pollution in the region are increasing the rate at which water resources are lost. Agriculture is by far the most important water use activity, but it is also one of the least efficient sectors in water use. Outdated irrigation techniques and skewed water pricing have allowed for the continued inefficient dominance of agriculture in water use. This poor water management contributes to increasing water scarcity, and thus to the increasing vulnerability to drought.

Drought in the ESCWA region also assumes an international dimension, as the region's three major waterways cross national boundaries. The difficulties in managing shared water resources in the region are magnified by the fact that the majority of the rainfall feeding these waterways originates outside the region. In addition, threats posed by cyclical drought compound water scarcity and increase regional competition.

It should be noted that Jordan, the Syrian Arab Republic and Yemen, the subjects of the above-mentioned case-studies presented herein, represent those countries in the ESCWA region whose rural/agricultural populations are comparatively high, and whose current access to freshwater resources is limited.

Jordan. From 1995 to 2001, Jordan endured mild to severe drought conditions. The 1998/99 agricultural season, one of the driest on record, led to a sharp drop in dam water levels, greatly reducing agricultural production. Rainfall in 1999 dropped by as much as 70 per cent in some zones of the country, resulting in agricultural yields and production that were the worst recorded in four decades. The drought reduced wheat and barley production in 1999 by 88 per cent. This, in turn, had serious repercussions on the rural populations dependent on the agricultural sector; as incomes fell sharply, assets were liquidated, and livestock herds were lost to disease, malnutrition, premature slaughter and distress sales. The economy, squeezed by the United Nations trade embargo on Iraq and the loss of the markets of the Gulf States as well as by regional conflicts, was unable to absorb the shock of drought. Limited off-farm economic opportunities and high rates of unemployment reduced the economy's capacity to absorb rural-urban labour migration. Moreover, the 1999 fall in foreign currency revenues and heavy foreign debt repayments limited Jordan's capacity to import the shortfall in agricultural production.

Syrian Arab Republic. The 1999-2001 drought greatly affected crop and livestock production in the Syrian Arab Republic, which, in turn, had serious repercussions on the food security of a large segment of the population, particularly among the small farmers and herders. Owing to a decrease in flow of the Euphrates River, irrigation canals dried up, and the country's hydro-powered electricity plants were unable to operate at capacity. Economic growth was affected as agricultural production fell sharply, reducing agricultural income contribution to gross domestic product (GDP). Although the Government made extensive efforts to reduce the effects of the drought, its scale and severity were such that the measures taken were inadequate. The drought coincided with an economic lull caused by the falling oil prices, which reduced both the country's resilience to drought and its ability to mitigate the effects thereof.

Yemen. The 1990/91 drought had a great impact on the Yemeni economy and population. As agricultural production fell sharply, economic growth was affected by the reduction of agricultural income's contribution to GDP. The agricultural sector registered significant yield losses, resulting in widespread farm losses and increased poverty in rural areas. The drought highlighted the vital role that adequate rainfall and water resources play in keeping Yemen's economy profitable and sustainable, as Yemen has no perennial rivers, and depends on rainfall from wadi run-off and groundwater recharge. The drought had serious repercussions on the food security of a large segment of the population. According to the World Bank, a sizeable portion of the population remains economically vulnerable to falling into poverty due to drought, as the Yemeni agricultural sector provides employment for 58 per cent of the population and a livelihood for 77 per cent.

Damaging droughts of recent years in the ESCWA region have increased awareness of the need for greater drought mitigation and preparedness measures. To that end, many Governments of the region have taken steps to develop drought preparedness capacity. Nevertheless, the region still lacks an expanded awareness of drought and its impacts, as well as the capacity to mitigate drought. Although the countries in the ESCWA region possess well-equipped meteorological networks, a lack of adequate drought monitoring institutions, tools and information-production and sharing has limited national capacities to predict and prepare for drought. As witnessed in the 1999-2001 drought, a large section of the region was affected, each country differently, in large part owing to differences in societal vulnerability to drought. Therefore, regional drought research should examine the ways in which non-climatic factors affect societal vulnerability to drought, and how drought planning and mitigation can help to reduce drought vulnerability. There is a need in the region to (a) build institutional and technical capacity; (b) harmonize and monitor socio-economic drought methodologies and indicators; (c) monitor drought and conduct regional vulnerability assessments; (d) develop drought preparedness strategies and early warning systems; and (e) reduce vulnerability through integrated policy planning.

CONTENTS

CONTENTS (*continued*)

LIST OF ABBREVIATIONS

ACC	Agriculture Credit Corporation
AMS	American Meteorological Society
AREA	Agriculture Research And Extension Authority (Yemen)
BOD	Biochemical Oxygen Demand
CIHEAM	International Centre for Advanced Mediterranean Agronomic Studies
DEWS	Drought Early Warning System
ENSO	El Niño Southern Oscillation
EO	Earth Observatory
EWFIS	Early Warning and Food Information System
FAO	Food and Agriculture Organization of the United Nations
FIVIMS	Food Insecurity and Vulnerability Information and Mapping Systems
GAP	Southern Anatolia Development Project
GCC	Gulf Cooperation Council
GDP	gross domestic product
GNP	gross national product
GIEWS	Global Information and Early Warning System on Food and Agriculture
GIS	Geographic Information Systems
ha	hectare
HDI	Human Development Index
HPI	Human Poverty Index
IAMZ	Mediterranean Agronomic Institute of Zaragoza
ICARDA	International Center for Agricultural Research in the Dry Areas
IDIC	International Drought Information Center
IFRC	International Federation of Red Cross and Red Crescent Societies
IPCC	Intergovernmental Panel on Climate Change
ISDR	International Strategy for Disaster Reduction
IUCN	International Union for the Conservation of Nature and Natural Resources
IWRM	Integrated Water Resources Management
JICA	Japan International Cooperation Agency
MENA	Middle East and North Africa
MIS	management information systems
NARS	National Agricultural Research Systems
NCARTT	National Center for Agricultural Research and Technology Transfer (Jordan)
NDMC	National Drought Mitigation Center
NEMEDCA	Network on Drought Management for the Near East, Mediterranean and Central Asia
NGO	non-governmental organizations
NWRA	National Water Resources Authority
NWSA	National Water and Sanitation Authority
PPEW	Platform for the Promotion of Early Warning
UNACC/SCWR	United Nations Administrative Committee on Coordination – Subcommittee on Water Resources
UNCCDD	United Nations Convention to Combat Desertification and Drought
UNDP	United Nations Development Programme
UNEP	United Nations Environment Programme
UNSO	UNDP Trust Fund to Combat Desertification and Drought
WFP	World Food Programme
WHO	World Health Organization
WMO	World Meteorological Organization
WRI	World Resources Institute
WTO	World Trade Organization
WUSI	water use sustainability indicator
WWAP	World Water Assessment Programme
WWDR	World Water Development Report

Introduction

At the urging of the Commission on Sustainable Development and with the strong endorsement of the Ministerial Conference on Water Security, held at The Hague in March 2000, the Administrative Committee on Coordination Subcommittee on Water Resources (UNACC/SCWR) undertook a collective United Nations system-wide continuing assessment process, the World Water Assessment Programme (WWAP).[1] Building on the achievements of the previous endeavours, WWAP focuses on assessing the developing situation of freshwater throughout the world. The primary output of WWAP is the periodic World Water Development Report (WWDR). Among other things, the role of WWAP is to identify water crises and thus provide guidance for national decision makers and donor agencies. It also provides the knowledge and understanding upon which to base further capacity-building.

The first WWDR, published in 2003, contained scant information on the Western Asia region, one of the most arid areas in the world. The second Report, to be published in 2006, is also unlikely to include adequate information on the region despite efforts by the Economic and Social Commission for Western Asia with the coordinating agencies. Moreover, because of weak coordination between the 23 United Nations bodies (UN Water) involved in the World Water Assessment Programme (WWAP), it is likely to be some time before the issues raised in the World Water Development Report can be presented in a balanced form reflecting national and regional water challenges within the global context.

In the light of the above, the ESCWA secretariat decided to initiate a series of development reports focused on the water issues of the region. Theme 9, on Management Challenges of the World Water Development Report 2, has been selected as the subject of the first ESCWA Water Development Report, with a special focus on drought management. Since UN Water is currently preparing for the World Water Development Report 3, it is hoped that the findings of this first ESCWA Water Development Report will be taken into account by World Water Development Report 3 with regard to reporting on the ESCWA region. More important, it is believed that this information will prove to be useful for the member States that are in the process of preparing comprehensive national integrated water resources management (IWRM) plans.

The sustainable development and management of water resources are not only exposed to extreme events generated as part of natural climatic changes, but are also linked to socio-economic and political factors as well as human error. Natural and human-induced hazards have become a major challenge to the management, protection and conservation of water resources, particularly in the ESCWA region which is recurrently affected by frequent disasters due to severe aridity, both fast (floods) and slow (droughts) events. To combat such disasters, management approaches that build on defined responsibility and timely, risk-based decision-making are needed.

Despite the vulnerability of the ESCWA region to recurrent droughts, there is to date no regional strategy or action plan for drought preparedness. Furthermore, most efforts involving ESCWA member countries have been concentrated on strengthening early warning systems for detecting meteorological and agricultural drought or responding to drought impacts under emergency conditions. Assessments of hydrological drought are correlated with agricultural drought indicators, particularly in irrigated crop areas. Hydrological drought management and preparedness are also inherently linked to geopolitical issues arising from shared water management in the ESCWA region, since nearly 70 per cent of the region's annual renewable freshwater resources originate in non-ESCWA member countries.

In view of the need to assist ESCWA member States to better prevent and manage drought from an integrated perspective, this study: (a) examines the various components of socio-economic drought; (b) identifies indicators and maps socio-economic drought vulnerability in the ESCWA region; and (c) proposes guidelines for incorporating socio-economic aspects in drought preparedness and mitigation in the region. The findings of this study will be shared with those engaged in drought mitigation and planning

---

[1] The ACC Subcommittee on Water Resources has been replaced by UN Water as the official United Nations system-wide mechanism for coordinating activities in the area of water resources.

in the ESCWA region, as well as with stakeholders that have been traditionally excluded from the decision-making process on issues related to drought prevention and preparedness.

In order to examine the socio-economic impacts of drought, this report will describe measures taken on drought management and mitigation in three regional case-studies on Jordan, the Syrian Arab Republic and Yemen. The three countries in the case-studies represent those countries in the ESCWA region whose rural/agricultural populations are comparatively high, and whose current access to freshwater resources is limited. In focusing on these three representative countries, the aim of this study is to draw conclusions on the impact of socio-economic drought on the region as a whole and to developing guidelines for drought mitigation and for a Drought Early Warning System (DEWS). It should be noted that, according to the data available to ESCWA, 43 per cent of the population in the region currently live in rural areas. The ESCWA members can be classified into two main categories:

(a) ESCWA members with < 20 per cent rural population: Bahrain (6 per cent), Kuwait (4 per cent), Qatar (6 per cent), Saudi Arabia (12 per cent), United Arab Emirates (11 per cent), and Lebanon (9 per cent);

(b) ESCWA members with > 20 per cent rural population: Egypt (57 per cent), Iraq (32 per cent), Jordan (21 per cent), Oman (21 per cent), Palestine (32 per cent), Syrian Arab Republic (47 per cent), and Yemen (74 per cent).

Of the seven ESCWA members with a relatively large rural population, two receive large supplies of freshwater through major rivers flowing into the region from more humid areas (Egypt and Iraq). The other five are essentially spread along the northern (Jordan, Palestine and the Syrian Arab Republic) and southern (Oman and Yemen) boundaries of the Arabian Peninsula, one of the most arid regions in the world. Hence, rural populations living in these five countries, especially in the dry parts, have very limited access to freshwater and are among the most vulnerable to drought-related disasters. The focus of the case-studies is on the socio-economic aspects of droughts in these arid areas of the ESCWA region. Socio-economic droughts are assessed in Jordan, the Syrian Arab Republic and Yemen so that the lessons learned can be of benefit to other ESCWA members. The assessment in each case-study was undertaken on the basis of climate, water resources, agriculture, environment and socio-economic vulnerability.

I. VULNERABILITY OF THE ESCWA REGION TO DROUGHT

A. Drought as a Water-Related Disaster

Of all natural hazards, drought affects most people around the world, and its impacts are among the most devastating. The United Nations Inter-Agency Secretariat of the International Strategy for Disaster Reduction (ISDR) describes drought as one of the most intractable hazards for developing countries.[2] Sustainable development challenges associated with the prevention and management of drought are also the focus of chapter 12 of Agenda 21. In recent years, owing to population growth, soil degradation, increased desertification, and projected climate change scenarios, drought research and drought planning have become crucial to averting and mitigating drought disasters.

Drought is often difficult to define, as it is more visible and better understood from its impacts than from its causes. Nevertheless, drought is generally defined as a period of insufficient water resources initiated by reduced precipitation, resulting in a water shortage for some activity, group or environmental sector.[3] Although drought is a normal, recurrent feature of climate, an increase in the frequency of droughts globally has been linked to climate change. Whereas weather, such as high temperatures and winds, may exacerbate drought, weather is not its only cause.[4] A drought disaster is caused by the combination of both a climate hazard—the occurrence of the drought—and societal vulnerability.

The severity of drought emerges not only from the degree of rainfall deficiency over time, but also from human activity that increases the water demand. Population growth, increasing demand for water for irrigation, industry, and domestic use, all put pressure on water supplies which in turn increases vulnerability to drought. Societal factors such as poor land-use practices, conflicts, poverty, poor communication infrastructure and lack of drought-mitigation measures also further accelerate drought disasters.

Given its social, economic and environmental impacts, drought cannot be viewed solely as a physical phenomenon. Recent droughts in both developing and developed countries and the resulting economic, environmental, and social impacts have underscored the vulnerability of all societies to drought. Although deficiencies in rainfall can be scientifically measured, the impacts of drought on society and natural ecosystems are not easily quantified. Moreover, socio-economic drought is a new concept in the literature on drought and disaster planning. While the importance of vulnerability and risk assessment was highlighted in the paper prepared by the UNISDR Ad Hoc Discussion Group on Drought in 2001/2002,[5] socio-economic drought was not specifically mentioned. However, in their 2004 joint publication,[6] UNISDR and the World Meteorological Organization (WMO) recognized socio-economic drought as an independent classification. This illustrates the growing awareness and concern about socio-economic drought and the need to ensure that it is incorporated within the planning and management frameworks of Governments, networks and associated stakeholders concerned with drought in the ESCWA region.

B. Vulnerability of the ESCWA Region to Drought

The ESCWA region accounts for about 4.5 per cent of the world's population, but only 0.62 per cent of the world's freshwater resources.[7] Rapid population and economic growth coupled with finite and

---

[2] International Strategy for Disaster Reduction and World Meteorological Organization, *Water and Disasters: Be Informed and Be Prepared* (Geneva, 2004), p. 27.

[3] American Meteorological Society, "AMS policy statement on meteorological drought", 1996.

[4] National Drought Mitigation Center, "Spotting drought before it's too late", University of Nebraska-Lincoln, 2005.

[5] International Strategy for Disaster Reduction, *Drought: Living with Risk: An Integrated Approach to Reducing Societal Vulnerability to Drought; ISDR Ad Hoc Discussion Group on Drought* (Geneva, 2004).

[6] ISDR and WMO, *Water and Disasters*, p. 21.

[7] ESCWA, Federal Institute for Geosciences and Natural Resources, Germany (BGR) and Deutsche Gesellschaft für Technische Zusammenarbeit (GTZ), *Enhancing Negotiation Skills on International Water Issues in the ESCWA Region* (Beirut, 2004), p. 1.

decreasing freshwater resources have greatly reduced annual per capita freshwater resources, from 3,300 cubic metres (m³) in 1960 to 1,250 m³ in 1996 to 981 m³ in 2000.[8] Of the ten most water-scarce countries in the world, eight ESCWA members top the list.[9] Most countries in the region live on average per capita water consumption levels well under the water poverty level of 1,000 m³ per person per year.[10] Of all the regions of the world, the Middle East faces the most daunting water resource challenges; as demand increases, water becomes more scarce and its quality declines. Thus vulnerability to drought in the ESCWA region becomes ever more pronounced.

The ESCWA region is characterized by considerable diversity in climatic conditions, with widely differing climatic regimes, ranging from humid to hyper-arid. In addition, temperature regimes vary considerably owing to differences in altitude and oceanic/coastal influences. The result is that almost all countries show a high degree of aridity in large parts of their territories, thereby increasing the region's vulnerability to drought and desertification.[11] For example, 50.9 per cent of Egypt's territory is classified as very dry, compared with 55.6 per cent in Jordan and 61.4 per cent in the Syrian Arab Republic.[12] Nevertheless, Egypt and the Syrian Arab Republic are among the least water-scarce per capita nations in the ESCWA region, and all three countries engage in considerable agricultural activity.

Recent studies have shown that global climate change is likely to exacerbate drought and desertification, particularly in the ESCWA region, where growing water scarcity places stress on economic activities, the environment and the region's biodiversity. This is evidenced by the increased frequency of drought episodes in the past two decades in the region, which has caused water tables to drop, shallow wells to dry up, and aquifers to reach their lowest levels in decades. Within a context in which there are few or no additional freshwater resources to tap, where existing water resource levels are exploited beyond their sustainable levels, and rainfall variability is pronounced in large parts of its territories, the population is thereby highly vulnerable to drought.

This vulnerability of ESCWA members to drought has intensified owing to the region's demographic and economic growth, increasing water scarcity, and land-use patterns. Poor land-use practices, such as overgrazing, over-cultivating and poor irrigation, have degraded and changed land characteristics, and this in turn has altered the general regional climate.[13] The result is reduced rainfall and general environmental degradation, which prompts desertification and increases drought vulnerability. In addition, water over-exploitation and pollution in the region increase water scarcity and reduce the ability of the region to mitigate drought impacts, thus increasing vulnerability to drought.

Further contributing to the water scarcity crisis is the inefficient allocation of scarce water resources. In the ESCWA region, agriculture is by far the most important water use activity, but is also one of the least efficient sectors in water use: outdated irrigation techniques and skewed water pricing have allowed for the continued inefficient dominance of agriculture in water use.[14] Water mismanagement in the region is not limited to the agricultural sector, however. Water losses in municipal distribution systems often exceed

---

[8] Ibid.

[9] World Bank, "Water Scarcity in the Middle East and North Africa", (Washington, DC, 2005) in *Enhancing Negotiation Skills on International Water Issues of the ESCWA Region*, p. 1.

[10] The World Bank sets water scarcity per capita at 1,000 m³ per capita per year, (World Bank, *World Development Report 1992: Development and the Environment*, 10517, May 1992).

[11] E. DePauw, "Drought early warning systems in West Asia and North Africa" (ICARDA, Syrian Arab Republic, 2004), p. 68.

[12] Ibid.

[13] IUCN Centre for Mediterranean Cooperation and Global Water Partnership - Mediterranean, "Drought Preparedness and Risk Management in the Mediterranean Region", paper by T.A. El Hassani presented at Water, Wetlands and Climate Change: Building Linkages for their Integrated Management, Mediterranean Regional Roundtable, held at Athens in 2002 (Gland, Switzerland, International Union for the Conservation of Nature and Natural Resources, 2002).

[14] ESCWA, BGR and GTZ, *Enhancing Negotiation Skills on International Water Issues in the ESCWA Region*.

50 per cent.[15] Poor water management policies also contribute to increasing water scarcity, and thus the increasing vulnerability to drought of the populations of the region.

Drought in the ESCWA region also assumes an international dimension, as the region's three major waterways (the Nile, the Jordan and Tigris-Euphrates Rivers) and other smaller river basins often cross national boundaries.[16] Water resources within many of the region's watersheds and river basins are shared by multiple nations, and challenges in managing shared water resources are compounded by the fact that the majority of the rainfall feeding these waterways originates outside the region, which provokes competition for, and may cause conflict over, these shared water resources. In that context, and since drought-induced water scarcity increases the urgent need for access to adequate water supplies, drought preparedness becomes a vital component of national and regional integrated water resource management.

C. STATE OF DROUGHT PREPAREDNESS AND MITIGATION IN THE ESCWA REGION

A number of measures have been taken by regional and international organizations to support the development of a drought early warning system (DEWS), particularly in dry land areas. Work at the international level is coordinated with the Food and Agriculture Organization of the United Nations (FAO) through the Global Information and Early Warning System on Food and Agriculture (GIEWS) and WMO. Regional networks have also been established to support capacity-building and information exchange among governments. For instance, the Network on Drought Management for the Near East, Mediterranean and Central Asia (NEMEDCA Drought Network) was launched in 2001 by FAO, the International Center for Agricultural Research in Dry Areas (ICARDA) and the International Centre for Advanced Mediterranean Agronomic Studies (CIHEAM) in an effort to contribute to the development and coordination of drought preparedness and mitigation plans and to promote the use of impact assessment tools.

However, national drought preparedness plans and drought early warning systems are generally non-existent or non-operational in the ESCWA region.[17] A limited level of information and of coordination on the extent and impact of drought from national sources, such as the water supply and irrigation authorities, agricultural extension services, meteorological departments, and non-governmental organizations (NGOs), has resulted in a lack of coordinated policy on drought and drought mitigation and preparedness measures. Although the countries in the region have well-equipped meteorological networks and systems, inadequate drought monitoring tools and insufficient information sharing have severely limited national capacities to predict and prepare for drought.[18] As the ESCWA region is the most arid region in the world, the need for drought mitigation and preparedness, as well as for a drought early warning system, is therefore critical.

The concentration on monitoring and responding to drought, rather than on establishing mitigation measures and drought early warning systems, has resulted in a gap in capacity and information regarding the detection, prevention, preparedness and mitigation of socio-economic drought in the ESCWA region. The inclusion of socio-economic dimensions in regional drought preparedness planning is essential to ensuring that integrated and sustainable approaches are adopted. This is particularly critical today as drought events in the region are becoming more frequent and severe,[19] and their impacts more widely felt in those ESCWA members with recurrent drought conditions, namely Jordan, Palestine, Syrian Arab Republic, Oman, United Arab Emirates and Yemen.

The gap in the understanding of socio-economic drought is also an outcome of difficulties associated with integrated planning and management in the ESCWA region. Socio-economic assessment and mitigation of drought require indicators, tools and policy approaches that are distinct from those pursued by traditional

---

[15] Ibid., p. 2.

[16] Ibid.

[17] E. DePauw, "Drought early warning systems in West Asia and North Africa".

[18] Ibid.

[19] IUCN, "Drought Preparedness and Risk Management in the Mediterranean Region", paper presented by T.A. El Hassani at the Mediterranean Regional Roundtable, p. 7.

agricultural and water resources professionals. For instance, socio-economic drought is commonly generated by dysfunctional markets and distorted prices for agricultural inputs and commodities,[20] with the impacts exacerbated under drought conditions.

Furthermore, while early warning detection systems are based on ensuring effective monitoring of a specific set of indicators associated with primary effects caused by rainfall or water resources, socio-economic indicators are often associated with secondary impacts. Traditionally, risk and vulnerability assessments have thus accounted for socio-economic impacts of drought by estimating the impact on food production, food security and nutrition. However, a wide range of other indicators should also be considered and adapted to regional and local circumstances if socio-economic implications are to be adequately reflected in planning decisions. These might include: availability and access to drinking water; sanitation; livestock protection (including fodder for livestock); employment opportunities;[21] agricultural and non-agricultural household income in rural areas; food prices as related to rural and urban household expenditures on food; and population migration patterns and trends.

Environmental indicators should also be included in view of the efforts to promote integrated development planning. While early warning systems and indicators have been developed and supported by geographic information systems (GIS) to monitor migrating pests and land degradation, other indicators should also be relied on to promote sustainable livelihoods. These might include indicators to monitor desertification, dust storms, sand movement and encroachment, as well as biodiversity, wildlife, wetlands and sensitive ecosystems. In view of these environmental dimensions, it should also be recognized that while climate change, desertification and drought are interrelated conditions, each has its own characteristics and requires preparedness plans and mitigation strategies that operate along different time lines.

---

[20] Ibid., p. 14.

[21] Ibid., p. 9.

II. CONCEPTUAL FRAMEWORK

A. DROUGHT TYPOLOGIES

Drought exists in several forms: meteorological drought; agricultural drought; hydrological drought; and socio-economic drought.

1. *Meteorological drought*

Meteorological drought is defined by the degree of dryness in comparison with the average for a region, and the duration of the dry period.[22] Meteorological droughts are by definition region-specific, as the levels of precipitation and duration of dryness must be compared with the regional norms. Even within regions, considerable variations in atmospheric conditions result in deficiencies of precipitation, and there is a wide range of time scales over which a meteorological drought can occur. Although crops can be damaged by a lack of precipitation over a few weeks at critical stages of growth, usually such short periods are not considered droughts. Meteorological drought is measured in terms of seasons, years, or decades of deficient precipitation. The duration of drought has a large impact on soil moisture and stream-flow, water supply in streams, shallow groundwater tables, and small lakes and reservoirs.[23] Thus, a short but severe drought may have more extensive impacts than a longer-lived drought that is less severe.

2. *Agricultural drought*

Agricultural drought links various characteristics of meteorological drought to agricultural impacts.[24] It occurs when there is insufficient soil moisture to meet the needs of a particular crop at a particular time.[25] Agricultural drought is complex in that its impacts depend on the magnitude, duration and timing of the drought, as well as on the responses of the region's soils, plants and animals to water stress. Insufficient topsoil moisture due to drought at planting may hinder germination, leading to low plant populations per hectare (ha) and a reduction of final yield. A drought occurring in the later stage of crop development can destroy or deplete crop yields. Alternatively, the actual impact of drought on agricultural crops depends on the biological characteristics of the crops, stage of growth, and the physical and biological properties of the soil.

3. *Hydrological drought*

Hydrological drought is generally defined on a watershed or river basin scale and measures the effects of periods of deficient precipitation on surface or subsurface water supply, such as stream flow, and on reservoir, lake and groundwater levels.[26] Although all droughts originate with a deficiency of precipitation, hydrological drought refers to deficiencies in water supply caused by rainfall deficiencies over the watershed or river basin. Hydrological droughts generally lag behind meteorological and agricultural droughts, as it takes longer for precipitation deficiencies to show up in components of the hydrological system.[27] When precipitation is below average for a long period of time, this is evidenced in declining surface and subsurface water levels, which may vary considerably, based on differing water uses. For example, a hydrological drought may not affect hydroelectric power production or recreational uses for many months, while a decrease in soil moisture levels will have an immediate impact on agriculture.

---

[22] National Drought Mitigation Center, "What is drought?" University of Nebraska-Lincoln, 2005.

[23] American Meteorological Society, "AMS policy statement on meteorological drought".

[24] Ibid.

[25] Earth Observatory, *Drought: The Creeping Disaster* (Florida, National Aeronautics and Space Administration [NASA], 2005).

[26] American Meteorological Society, "AMS policy statement on meteorological drought".

[27] National Drought Mitigation Center, "Spotting drought before it's too late".

4. *Socio-economic drought*

Socio-economic drought occurs when water supply is insufficient to meet human and environmental needs, and emerges when a meteorological, hydrological, or agricultural drought adversely affects the supply and demand of economic goods. Since socio-economic drought occurs when inadequate rainfall causes a decrease in the production of goods and services, it can be thought of, for example, as drought-triggered food insecurity.[28] Thus, socio-economic impacts of drought disasters can be a serious obstacle to the development of many less developed countries with losses equivalent to several years of national growth gains.[29] Owing to competing and different water uses, conflict over priority of water uses during a drought also assumes a socio-economic dimension. On a watershed or river basin scale, water users may not only represent different and competing sectors of the economy, but also different nations sharing the water resources as well as the water shortage. In these cases, drought takes on a complicated international dimension, and competition escalates during drought, as do conflicts between water users in which the poor and voiceless are often the first to succumb to the adverse impacts of the drought.

B. ASSESSING DROUGHT VULNERABILITY

Vulnerability to drought is complex, yet it is important to understand in order to design effective drought preparedness plans and mitigation strategies. Vulnerability of communities to drought is dependent on physical, social, environmental and economic characteristics. In the past, drought monitoring and research focused almost exclusively on the relation of climatic patterns and rainfall deficiencies to water supply and water resource levels. However, this approach did not examine how human water use can also exacerbate deficits in water supply, reliability, and quality, and result in multiplying the negative impacts of a meteorological drought. Drought vulnerability research examines how drought impacts result from interactions of social, political, and economic systems, as well as the meteorological drought phenomenon.[30]

1. *Characteristics of drought vulnerability*

(a) *Physical characteristics* which increase drought vulnerability are: (i) highly variable hydrological and climatic regimes that are marginal for agricultural and livestock development; (ii) episodic precipitation patterns that produce high sedimentation and siltation rates; (iii) topography and soil patterns that promote soil erosion; and (iv) consistent regional climatic conditions that weaken relocation strategies as a drought mitigation measure;[31]

(b) *Social characteristics* contributing to drought vulnerability are: (i) low income levels; (ii) poverty; (iii) wars and conflicts; (iv) pandemics; (v) high dependence on rain-fed systems; (vi) high population densities, which hinder population mobility and relocation strategies; (vii) remoteness of drought-affected populations; and (viii) inexperience of communities in coping with drought;[32]

(c) *Economic characteristics* contributing to increased drought vulnerability include: (i) high dependence on domestic agro-production for food security; (ii) low export earnings that could be used to import food during a drought; (iii) high economic and labour force concentration in agriculture; (iv) low economic diversification; and (v) general instability in balance of payments;

---

[28] UNDP-DDC/BCPR and UN-ISDR, *Drought Risk and Development* Policy, Discussion paper for the UNDP-DDC/BCPR and UN-ISDR Expert Workshop, 31 January - 2 February 2005, Nairobi.

[29] Ibid.

[30] CLIMAS, "Drought planning and mitigation: social vulnerability", Climate Assessment for the Southwest, The Institute for the Study of Planet Earth, University of Arizona, 2004.

[31] UNEP, *Environmental Emergencies News*, issue 2 (Nairobi, United Nations Environmental Programme, February 2004).

[32] Ibid.

(d) *Political characteristics* that increase vulnerability to drought stem primarily from inadequate policies and poor governance in water resource management, and include: (i) lack of drought preparedness plans; (ii) lack of regional watershed or basin-wide shared water resource management agreements; (iii) ineffective integrated water resources management policies and institutions; (iv) inability to bolster non-precipitation-dependent water supplies for crucial water uses such as power generation and irrigation; and (v) poor management of water resources, particularly for agricultural purposes;

(e) *Environmental factors* contributing to increased vulnerability to drought include: (i) progressing desertification; (ii) high rates of soil erosion, over-cultivation, and overgrazing; and (iii) fragile ecosystems.

2. *Risk, vulnerability and impact assessment*

Each type of drought produces a unique set of impacts, depending not only on its severity and duration, but also on a society's social, economic and environmental conditions. Risk is defined by the extent of exposure to drought and the vulnerability of the location and its population to periods of drought-induced water shortages. Since a range of social, physical, environmental and economic factors shape society's vulnerability, impacts extend beyond the area physically affected by drought and can linger after the event has ended. Drought impact assessment examines the consequence of a drought, and begins by identifying its direct impacts, such as reduced crop yields, livestock losses, and reservoir depletion, and linking them to secondary effects, such as income loss, unemployment, forced migration, or famine.

Tools and methods. Although there are no standardized indicators and methodology to measure drought vulnerability and impact, several tools and methodologies do exist. International agencies such as the International Federation of Red Cross and Red Crescent Societies (IFRC) have developed vulnerability and capacity assessment for natural hazard risk assessment, including drought. Moreover, several national and sub-national governments have developed step-by-step hazard risk and vulnerability analysis toolkits for emergency planners and policy makers.[33] A current, region-specific and prioritized drought impact analysis will reveal sectors, populations, or activities that are most vulnerable to drought and that, when evaluated with the probability of drought occurrence, will identify drought vulnerability. A key dimension of drought risk impact assessments is the presentation of the results. An effective tool in increasing understanding of drought risk and vulnerability impact assessments is hazard mapping, which highlights geographic areas, economic sectors and populations at risk.

Gap. Vulnerability assessments and drought risk-mapping require interdisciplinary research involving social and natural sciences, engineering and management professionals and institutions at the local, district/municipal and national levels to best determine how to act on information about the availability of water and the effects of drought. However, integrating interdisciplinary data into a drought early warning system and generating operational drought-impact assessments are often hindered by lack of institutional, technical and financial capacity, and by a deficiency of inter-institutional communication.

Worldwide, there is a shortage of effective disaster preparedness and mitigation methods owing to the fact that risk reduction is not an integral part of water resource management.[34] Many countries have neither drought preparedness and mitigation plans, nor designated authorities to conduct drought impact assessments and preparedness strategies. Moreover, drought risk and vulnerability assessments and the consequent early warning systems must be mainstreamed into development planning to be effective. As such, the question of drought preparedness and mitigation is as much a question of governance as it is of the technical capacity of meteorological services, and of the integration of multidisciplinary data.

---

[33] Examples include the Provincial Emergency Program of British Columbia, the Canada Hazard Risk and Vulnerability Analysis Tool Kit, and the United States National Oceanic and Atmospheric Administration community vulnerability assessment step-by-step guide.

[34] ISDR. *Living with Risk: A Global Review of Disaster Reduction Initiatives* (Geneva, Inter-Agency Secretariat of the United Nations International Strategy for Disaster Reduction, 2004).

C. REVIEW OF EXISTING DROUGHT PREPAREDNESS
AND MITIGATION STRATEGIES

In the past two decades, droughts have occurred with increasing frequency, with recent studies indicating that climate change is likely to exacerbate the situation further. It is within this context that drought issues have gained attention and that drought preparedness strategies have been promoted, above all in the developing world where drought vulnerability is tied to economic diversification and growth. In 1991, the Wilhite drought planning methodology was developed in the United States and has since gained widespread adherence (see annex II to this study).[35] The goal of this process is to derive a plan that is dynamic and reflects changing government policies, technologies, and natural resource management practices. It is intended for use by planners as a checklist to identify issues that need to be addressed in plan development.

Current efforts seek to monitor, collect and disseminate information on drought indicators and convey information to the appropriate channels. Work at the international level is coordinated with FAO, through GIEWS, and WMO, with world food prices monitored to estimate supply and demand. At the national level, GIEWS monitors 80 Low-Income-Food-Deficit Countries through the National Food Balance Sheet, which monitors commercial imports, including food aid delivery, in order to estimate the amount of food needed to maintain food consumption at normal levels.[36] At the sub-national level, GIEWS monitors vulnerable populations and indicators of food crisis involving local food supply and prices, malnutrition levels and migration patterns.[37]

In many drought-vulnerable areas of Africa, FAO has also established Early Warning and Food Information System (EWFIS) to monitor food security,[38] whereby national units collect, process and communicate information using a well-established methodology of assessment based on crop condition and food security monitoring. However, in the ESCWA region, GIEWS and EWFIS, essentially food security monitoring systems used to detect and prevent drought-induced famines, have not yet been established.[39]

Constraints of socio-economic drought preparedness and mitigation

One of the key flaws of the current early warning systems is that they are intended to measure the food security outlook and vulnerability, not drought. "Food security" early warning systems are useful in avoiding famine situations in areas such as Africa, where food insecurity is endemic. However, in other regions where drought, not food insecurity, has been the chief issue, food security early warning systems have been of little use.[40] The inclusion of social, environmental and economic variables in drought assessments and drought early warning systems remains a major challenge to drought planners.[41] This is due to the limited development of common reporting and data collection standards, and the lack of effective methods for capturing economic losses, socio-economic behavioural changes, and coping mechanisms of communities affected by drought.[42]

---

[35] D.A. Wilhite and M.D. Svoboda, "Drought early warning systems in the context of drought preparedness and mitigation" (Lincoln, Nebraska, National Drought Mitigation Center, 2000).

[36] E. DePauw, "Drought early warning systems in West Asia and North Africa".

[37] Ibid.

[38] Ibid.

[39] Ibid.

[40] Ibid.

[41] United Nations International Strategy for Disaster Reduction, *Living with Risk: A Global Review of Disaster Reduction Initiatives*.

[42] United Nations Convention to Combat Desertification and Drought, "Early Warning Systems: report of the ad hoc Panel" (ICCD/COP (4)/CST/4), Conference of the Parties, Committee on Science and Technology, fourth session, Bonn, December 2000.

Drought monitoring and drought vulnerability analysis raise several technical and institutional challenges, since the technological infrastructure for data inputs and outputs is often lacking. In addition, a lack of technical understanding commonly exists between the bodies undertaking drought impact assessments and the policy makers.[43] One of the major impediments to drought planning is financial cost, since technology and institutional capacity to implement drought early warning systems are costly. These immediate and fixed costs of plans are often difficult to justify at the political level, given the unknown costs of a future drought.

---

[43] Ibid.

III. UNDERSTANDING SOCIO-ECONOMIC DROUGHT

A. COMPONENTS OF A SOCIO-ECONOMIC DROUGHT EARLY WARNING SYSTEM

TABLE 1. THE FOUR ELEMENTS OF EFFECTIVE EARLY WARNING SYSTEMS

Prior knowledge of the risks faced by communities	Technical monitoring and warning service for these risks	Dissemination of understandable warnings to those at risk	Knowledge and preparedness to act
Questions: Risks arise from both the hazards and the vulnerabilities that are present – what are the trends in these factors?	Questions: Is there a scientific basis for predicting the risks faced? Are the right things being monitored? Can accurate warnings be made in timely fashion?	Questions: Do the warnings get to those at risk? Do people understand them? Do they contain useful information that enables proper responses?	Questions: Do communities understand their risks? Do they respect the warning service? Do they know how to react?

Source: Platform for the Promotion of Early Warning, "Basics of early warning" (United Nations/International Disaster Reduction Strategy, 2005).

As shown in table 1 above, an effective early warning system comprises four elements with strong linkages between them. An integrated, multidisciplinary approach is necessary, as are regular and accurate data collection, monitoring and risk assessment.[44] Finally, information dissemination of risk assessment findings is the key to effective mitigation of drought impacts.

The components of a socio-economic drought early warning system are basically threefold: (a) data collection; (b) data integration and analysis; and (c) information dissemination or reporting. This section describes in more detail the components of a socio-economic drought early warning system.

1. *Indicators and thresholds*

Indicators and thresholds represent the conceptual content of the information to be produced within an early warning system. The overall aim of establishing a threshold is to assess the change in order to determine drought risk and vulnerability.[45] The variations in the different early warning systems are considerable and, as such, will yield differing results when compared with current data. Therefore, indicator thresholds should be region- or country-specific and modified to reflect market, climate, environment, public health and socio-economic changes.

Drought monitoring systems are critical to establish the probability of, and exposure to, drought. Meteorological tools identify various indicators of drought, track them, and provide a crucial means of monitoring, and hence assessing, drought risk. Meteorological monitoring systems are supplemented by crop monitoring systems, which rely on agro-meteorological models to determine crop stage and condition. Drought indices, measuring deviation of precipitation over a region over time, are then generated from a number of drought indicators. Moreover, in a socio-economic early warning system, the data are supplemented by social and economic indicators, including nutritional indices, behavioural indicators, and signals of economic activity[46] such as human and animal population and growth rate; water and fodder

---

[44] Platform for the Promotion of Early Warning, "Basics of early warning" (United Nations/International Strategy for Disaster Reduction, 2005).

[45] United Nations Convention to Combat Desertification and Drought, "Existing experience of early warning systems and specialized institutions in this field" (ICCD/COP(3)/CST/6), Conference of the Parties, Committee on Science and Technology, third session, Recife, October 1999, p. 31.

[46] R. Huss-Ashmore, "Local-level data for use as early warning indicators" (Philadelphia, University of Pennsylvania), Internet Journal of African Studies, vol. 2, March 1997.

requirements; severity of crop failure; industry types and their water requirements; income levels; food market prices; malnutrition rates; migration patterns; livestock sales; livestock mortality rates; and land degradation.

2. *Data management and sharing*

The timely collection of data entered into a socio-economic drought early warning system requires multi-tiered data coordination at the local, district/municipal, and national levels. Central coordination is necessary to ensure standardization of field data collection, while significant communication and collaboration between the relevant drought-monitoring and disaster-planning bodies is essential for the timely flow of information. Moreover, drought early warning systems require the participation of meteorological, agricultural, natural resource networks and professionals, as well as policy planners to best determine how to act on the information they receive about water availability and drought effects.

3. *Assessment and reporting*

Drought early warning system information requires processing within a drought impact assessment methodology, based on which risk scenarios are constructed and reviewed. The findings are distributed among policy planners for drought mitigation, as well as stakeholders including farmers, pastoralists and drought-threatened communities through channels such as radio, Internet, workshops, extension programmes, knowledge centres, and cultural and religious events. Provision of information for preparedness is an integral part of an early warning system and should be designed to help populations to prepare effectively for the risks and hazards associated with socio-economic drought.[47] However, there is often a gap in understanding between the bodies undertaking drought impact assessments and the policy makers, local authorities and communities receiving this information.[48] This can be overcome by strengthening people's capacity to understand, interpret and act on information through public information and education about the risk of and preparedness for drought.

In any early warning mechanism, there is always some degree of uncertainty about the predicted outcome. This is particularly true of the social components of an early warning, and the possible human impacts that might occur. This can make it difficult for decision makers to act, since they and those at risk must weigh the chances and consider the implications for their particular situation, including cost implications. For example, in the event of drought early warning, farmers must decide whether to plant drought-resistant seed, knowing it will not produce as much as the non-drought-resistant variety.[49] Accurate indicators for effective assessment of drought risk thus become crucial.

B. SOCIO-ECONOMIC DROUGHT INDICATORS

In the established drought early warning systems, climatic, meteorological and agricultural indicators and indices have been used to great effect. These include well-established indices such as the Percent of Normal, Standardized Precipitation Index, Palmer Drought Severity Index, Crop Moisture Index, Surface Water Supply Index, Reclamation Drought Index, and Deciles.[50] These indices are supplemented by satellite imagery, and the data are incorporated into various agro-meteorological models. The gap in socio-economic drought early warning systems, however, involves the incorporation of socio-economic data that accurately serve as predictors of socio-economic drought. As such, this section focuses on identifying possible socio-economic indicators to be used in regional socio-economic drought early warning systems.

---

[47] United Nations Convention to Combat Desertification, "Early warning systems: report of the ad hoc Panel", p. 7.

[48] United Nations International Disaster Reduction Strategy, *Living with Risk: A Global Review of Disaster Reduction Initiatives*.

[49] Platform for the Promotion of Early Warning, "Basics of early warning".

[50] M. Hayes, "What is drought? Drought indices", National Drought Mitigation Center, University of Nebraska-Lincoln, 2005.

1. Macroeconomic indicators

National income in drought tends to fall as water-dependent sectors are unable to perform owing to water shortages, which is particularly true of the agricultural sector, where falling agricultural production and income can be indicative of socio-economic drought. As such, the contribution of water-dependent sectors to GDP should be monitored as an early warning signal. Indicators in this category include: GDP for the agricultural sector; GDP contribution by sector (as a percentage of total); total agricultural production; agricultural production by crop; agricultural food production index; meat and milk production; feed costs; livestock resources; land in permanent crops; agricultural production (total area harvested); agricultural water use (as a percentage of total water withdrawals); and debt levels.

Economic diversity determines vulnerability or resilience to drought, since it allows an economy to stabilize the adverse effects of drought, particularly if there is significant economic diversity in non-water dependent sectors. Conversely, an undiversified economy will be less able to diffuse the adverse socio-economic impacts of a drought, particularly if the economy is heavily dependent on agriculture. Economic diversity as an indicator of drought vulnerability or resilience is applicable locally, nationally and regionally, and can be measured by the contribution of economic sectors to GDP; sources of GDP income; level of exports; diversity of economic activity; percentage of labour force by economic sector; unemployment rates; and wage rates by sector.

Labour force employment and migration can serve as a good measure of conditions in areas threatened by drought. Employment rates, although affected by a variety of conditions, can be an effective indicator of worsening drought-induced socio-economic conditions, particularly in agriculture-dependent economies. Labour force migration away from water-dependent sectors such as agriculture, and increased demand for non-agrarian employment, is generally indicative of worsening conditions in the agricultural sector. Increased unemployment will also be reflected in lowered per capita income, which in the case of water-dependent sectors can reveal socio-economic vulnerability by economic activity. Labour force drought indicators include: agricultural labour force as a percentage of total labour force; total agricultural labour force; agricultural labour force intensity; agricultural unemployment rate; Gini index; poverty rate; poverty gap; income per capita by sector; national savings; and rural-urban migration rates.

Trade and food security on the national scale, in terms of food balance sheets, volumes of crop sales, and market prices for crops and livestock, can provide data on aggregate food availability.[51] In addition, a country's exports in relation to its imports reflect the sustainability of the import bill, and its food security or its ability to increase food imports in case of drought. The indebtedness levels of a country may also reflect a country's ability to increase the import bill in cases of drought. Indicators include: debt/GDP and export/import ratios; percentage of agricultural exports; foreign exchange reserves; and crop and livestock yields.

2. Microeconomic indicators

While macro-level data are generally considered to be useful, they are unable to distinguish with sufficient lead-time those individual communities most in need of relief. The use of micro or local-level indicators has, therefore, been suggested to provide information on deteriorating economic conditions and food supply at the village or sub-district level.[52] Examples include:

Market activity at the local levels has been used to signal an impending food shortage. In general, two aspects have been monitored: amounts of grain or livestock being traded, and changes in the prices of these commodities. Indicators include stocks of cattle, chicken, camels, goats and sheep; livestock prices; volume and classes of livestock sales; prices of different grains; and core and food price index.

---

[51] R. Huss-Ashmore, "Local-level data for use as early warning indicators".

[52] Ibid.

Household income diversity, like economic diversity, is reflective of a household's vulnerability to drought. For example, rural households and communities that depend on few or interrelated economic activities as a source of income will be more vulnerable to drought. Conversely, a household with multiple sources of income, or with alternate employment possibilities, will be better able to alleviate the drought-induced income losses. Indicators in this category include unemployment rates by district; road networks; sources of household income and wealth; seasonal income; income levels; workers' remittances; savings; and debt.

Food as a share of household expenditures can reflect changes in food supply as well as changes in income, whereby increased food spending as a share of expenditures shows increased vulnerability to drought. In addition, the composition of the household food basket is also indicative of worsening food supply and vulnerability to drought. Indicators in this category include food aid per capita; caloric supply per capita; food consumption by age group and gender; underweight children under 5; wasting in children under 5; and poverty gaps and rates.

Livestock herds generally decline in the case of drought, as families liquidate livestock assets to gain income, and herders may have to sell classes of animals such as pregnant females that would not normally be put up for sale, in order to meet short-term food security needs. Distress sales of livestock may result in a rapid drop in the market price of herd animals. As such, monitoring levels of livestock sales, prices, classes, mortality rate, density, and malnutrition are also good socio-economic drought indicators.

3. *Population and gender dimensions*

Income distribution among quintiles can indicate worsening socio-economic conditions for the lower quintiles. The poor generally have a smaller repertoire of alternatives available to them to cope with drought, both in terms of disposable assets and of networks and food reserves. They are, therefore, more vulnerable than wealthier people to food shortage, and may reach the point of distress sales or migration earlier in the crisis and, as such, are a key population to monitor for early warning signals. Indicators include: poverty rate and gap; poverty rate by sector; income inequality; wages by sector; and coping mechanisms of the poor.

Social conflict often results from severe drought impacts on socio-economic conditions such as worsening food supply and economic options, and may be a useful indicator to determine the severity of socio-economic drought. Data on crime rates, conflict, rule of law, voice and accountability, unemployment-related violence, conflict-induced migration, refugee flows, and water flows originating from other countries can be good indicators of the social impacts of drought.

Age and gender alter the strategies available, their effectiveness, and the timing of their use in a developing drought crisis. In many countries, women and the elderly are among the first to alter their behaviour to cope with the adverse impacts of drought. Women tend to reduce food consumption. Similarly, the very young and the very old are more vulnerable. Children may drop out of school or be sent to eat or live with relatives. It is important to determine whose responses are the most reliable in terms of being the timeliest warning of drought, food shortage, and socio-economic crisis. Indicators include: school enrolment rates by gender, food consumption and nutrition by age group and gender, and school enrolment and death rates by district.

Migration patterns often indicate worsening socio-economic conditions as a result of drought, as populations migrate in search of employment, new water supplies and better socio-economic conditions. Rural-urban migration, as well as international emigration, may reflect worsening rural and agricultural socio-economic conditions. This migration may also place added pressure on government assistance, housing, resources, and services within urban centres. As such, indicators in this category may include: urban growth rate; conflict-induced migration; refugee flows; rural-urban migration patterns; government assistance by geographic region; and water-use intensity by geographic region.

4. *Health indicators*

Nutrition in a drought situation generally deteriorates for all affected groups. Household food consumption generally drops, and the core food basket changes to reflect lowered incomes, increased grain and feed prices, and availability of cheap alternatives. Vulnerable groups such as women and the elderly are generally first to reduce food intake. Livestock will also show signs of nutritional deficiencies early in a drought. Monitoring those groups first showing signs of nutritional deficiencies is crucial to early warning. Nutritional indicators include: weight-for-age or weight-for-height in children; calorie supply per capita; reduction of food consumption by gender and age group; calorie supply per capita from meat products; wasting in children under 5; malnutrition in children under 5; stunting, average birth-weight of infants; and livestock diseases and malnutrition.

Access to safe drinking water and sanitation is another key indicator of general public health. Drought reduces the availability of water and can adversely affect health, as levels of hygiene drop and availability of safe drinking water falls. Per capita water consumption below the "basic human water right" level of 180 m^3 per person per year represents a health risk. Sanitation in a drought situation generally deteriorates as low water flows increase cross-connection contamination and increase pollutant concentrations. Indicators in this category include: access to improved water source (rural and urban); water quality; pollution concentrations; sewage flows; cross-connection contamination; access to improved sanitation (urban and rural); waterborne diseases; and per capita domestic water consumption.

5. *Environmental indicators*

Land degradation increases vulnerability to drought as ecosystems, pasturelands and forestlands shrink and become less productive while desertification increases. Increased pressure on land and water resources reduces their productive capacity and susceptibility to drought. Increased fertilizer use and increased water use intensity may compensate for decreasing soil productivity, and hence are good indicators with regard to land degradation. Similarly, the area of cropland per capita is a good indicator of the pressure on land resources. Other indicators include: changes in stream flow and water levels; desertification rates; irrigation levels; number of groundwater wells; soil infiltration rates; evaporation rates; vegetation cover; and dust storms.

Biodiversity also suffers adverse impacts in a drought as water becomes scarce, and water-dependent ecosystems, such as wetlands and fish water habitats, shrink or disappear. Reduced productivity of pasturelands and forestlands, and increased tree disease and wildfires, adversely affect biodiversity. Indicators include: deforestation and desertification rates; abundance of wildlife; vegetation cover; number of threatened animal and plant species; ecosystem area; extent of dry land; productivity of forestland and pasturelands; water recharge rates; water levels; and stream flow.

Marginal ecosystems with low rainfall are among the most vulnerable to drought, and are often susceptible to widespread environmental deterioration, and loss of habitats and wildlife. Poor land-use patterns and drought have placed stress on rangelands, leading to increased desertification and loss of productivity and biodiversity. Indicators include: vegetation cover; incidence of dust storms; water table levels; desertification rates; ecosystem area; water recharge rates; abundance of wildlife; wind erosion; and soil productivity.

There are a number of indices and data sets that are in widespread use. It is important to understand clearly the strengths, weaknesses and biases of each indicator, as they are integrated into a socio-economic drought early warning system. A sample list of socio-economic and environmental indicators to be incorporated into a socio-economic drought early warning system can be found in annex III to this study.

IV. ASSESSING SOCIO-ECONOMIC DROUGHT IN THE
ESCWA REGION: VULNERABILITY

Drought is a recurring event in the ESCWA region and has intensified and become more frequent in the last decades due to climate change, and increased pressure on land and water resources. Droughts in the region have had significant impacts, particularly in the agricultural sector. In 1999, the ESCWA region suffered a severe drought, greatly reducing agricultural production and its contribution to GDP in many countries. For the Middle East region, FAO estimated that cereal output in 1999 declined 12 per cent below the previous five-year average, and cereal exports were estimated to have dropped more than 50 per cent, while cereal imports were estimated to increase by 13 per cent.[53] Drought has had a great impact on the agricultural sector at the national level too. For example, in Iraq, rainfall was 30 per cent below average, and the water level in the country's major rivers dropped by more than 50 per cent during the 1999 drought.[54] As a result, rain-fed agriculture experienced a 70 per cent failure in crop germination, and losses of wheat and barley production of 37 and 63 per cent, respectively, of the annual average in central and southern Iraq.[55]

Consequently, the economies in the ESCWA region are becoming more dependent on imported food items, making them more vulnerable to sharp rises in international market prices. Economic development in the ESCWA region remains dependent on growth in agriculture, particularly in the non-oil-exporting countries. As a result, droughts have not only reduced agricultural production and increased rural poverty, but have also affected economic growth. The following section outlines the region's vulnerability to drought.

A. CLIMATIC VULNERABILITY

According to the Johannesburg Plan of Implementation, the Western Asia region "is known for its scarce water and limited fertile land resources". The region contains widely differing climatic regimes, ranging from humid to hyper-arid (see figure I). Temperature regimes vary considerably, owing to differences in altitude and oceanic/coastal influences. The result is that the region has a high degree of precipitation fluctuations and aridity. The large fluctuations in precipitation, shown in figure II, combined with a high degree of aridity, result in increased vulnerability to drought.

Figure I. Aridity of Western Asia and North Africa

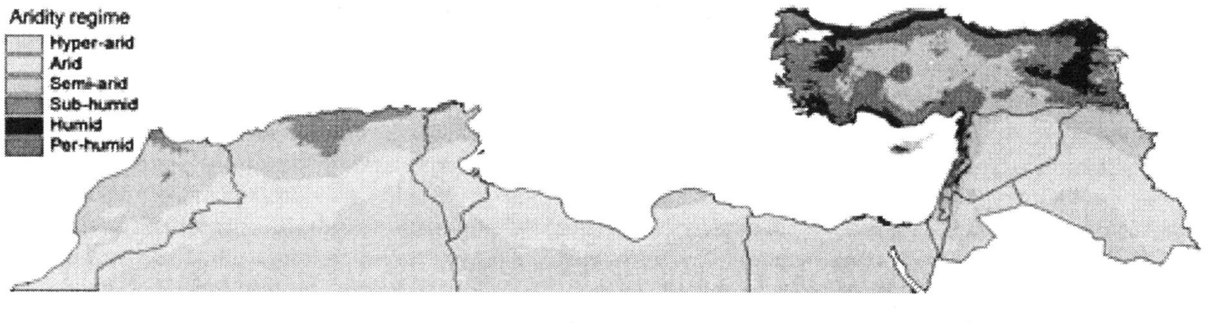

Source: E. DePauw, "Drought in WANA: six frequently asked questions", ICARDA *Caravan* 17, December 2002.

---

[53] FAO, "Drought in the Near East: cereal and livestock production down sharply", Global Watch, Rome, July 29, 1999.

[54] Ibid.

[55] FAO, "Adverse effects of the drought on domestic food production during 1998/1999 in Iraq", Food and Agriculture Organization of the United Nations in Iraq, Baghdad, May 1999, p. 16.

**Figure II. Precipitation fluctuations for three stations
under different moisture regimes, 1951-1985**

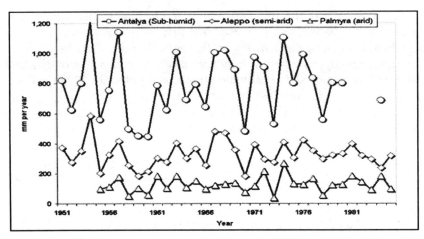

Source: E. DePauw, "Drought in WANA: six frequently asked questions", ICARDA *Caravan* 17, December 2002.

The patterns of drought in the region are extremely variable. Some droughts are severe enough to affect the entire region, and others are local. Weather patterns in many parts of the world appear to be related to different phases of the El Niño Southern Oscillation (ENSO) cycle, the linkages from which have been incorporated into drought early warning systems worldwide to predict rainfall patterns by season and assess the risk of drought. However, in the ESCWA region, no significant relationship between drought and ENSO events has been established to date.[56] For this reason, long-term forecasts based on ENSO linkages are not feasible, and drought becomes less predictable, thereby hindering early warning and increasing vulnerability to drought.

Mapping hot spots of drought vulnerability, based on remote sensing of the response of vegetation to weather fluctuations, is very useful for drought impact assessments. Figure III shows the spatial distribution of physical drought vulnerability in the northern ESCWA region.[57]

**Figure III. Spatial distribution of physical drought vulnerability in
Western Asia and North Africa**

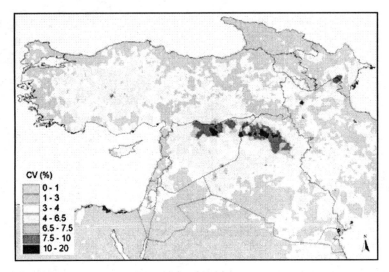

Source: E. DePauw, "Drought in WANA: six frequently asked questions", ICARDA *Caravan* 17, December 2002.

---

[56] E. DePauw, "Drought early warning systems in West Asia and North Africa".

[57] Ibid., "Drought in WANA: six frequently asked questions", ICARDA *Caravan* 17, December 2002.

B. WATER RESOURCE VULNERABILITY

The people in the following ESCWA members live below the critical water scarcity level of 500 m³ per year: Bahrain, Jordan, Kuwait, Palestine, Qatar, Saudi Arabia, United Arab Emirates and Yemen.[58] Current water demand trends and the unsustainable use of renewable water resources threaten the viability and water quality in groundwater aquifers, and opportunities for large captures of new water are now very few in the region. Drought exacerbates the situation by diminishing water replenishment rates, thereby reducing annual renewable water resources (table 2).

TABLE 2. RENEWABLE WATER RESOURCES IN ESCWA MEMBERS

ESCWA member	Total renewable water resources (*Millions of m³*)	Annual water use per capita 1997 (*m³*)	Water use intensity (*m³/ha/yr*) (*2000*)	Water use sustainability index (*WUSI*)*
Bahrain	100.2	173	28,333.3	309
Egypt	59,600	925	16,363.6	106
Iraq	62,850	2,963	7,108.3	78
Jordan	750	168	1,895.9	118
Kuwait	160.1	89	23,333.3	439
Lebanon	3,100	995	2,756.6	40
Oman	1,468	613	15,339.7	84
Qatar	51.4	98	10,047.6	564
Saudi Arabia	6,080	311	4,075.1	268
Syrian Arab Republic	21,475	1,438	3,536.5	46
United Arab Emirates	315	137	6,371.0	388
Palestinian territories	215	-	-	205
Yemen	4,900	303	3,786.3	55

Source: ESCWA, *Application of Sustainable Development Indicators in the ESCWA Member Countries: Analysis of Results* (2000), p. 22; and World Resources Institute, "EarthTrends Online Database", Washington, D.C., 2004.

* WUSI is the ratio of the amount of water used to the total renewable amount, calculated as a percentage.

Moreover, over-exploitation, inefficient water allocation and water pollution in the region are increasing the rate at which water resources are lost, thereby increasing drought vulnerability. For example, over-exploitation has led to the contamination of 80 per cent of the Gaza aquifer by the intrusion of seawater. In the region, agriculture is by far the most important water use activity, but is also one of the least efficient sectors in water use: outdated irrigation techniques and skewed water pricing have allowed for the continued inefficient dominance of agriculture in water use. It has been estimated that the irrigation of one ha of cropland in the ESCWA region requires 12,000 m³ of water, whereas the average in many other parts of the world is less than 7,500 m³.[59] Irrigation efficiency ranges from 30 to 50 per cent in most ESCWA member countries,[60] while water losses in municipal distribution systems in major cities of the region often exceed 50 per cent.[61] Application of the water use sustainability indicator (WUSI) to the ESCWA member States shows that Iraq, Lebanon, and the Syrian Arab Republic, the least water-poor countries of the region, had WUSIs reaching 68, 40 and 46 per cent respectively in 1997.[62] WUSIs above 40 per cent show water mismanagement, serious water scarcity, and the immediate need for intensive water management strategies.

---

[58] Ibid., p. 1.

[59] ESCWA, *Updating the Assessment of Water Resources in the ESCWA Member Countries* (1999), p. 60.

[60] Ibid.

[61] ESCWA, *Enhancing Negotiation Skills on International Water Issues in the ESCWA Region*, p. 2.

[62] ESCWA, *Updating the Assessment of Water Resources in ESCWA Member Countries*, p. 5.

In addition, the ESCWA region's three major waterways and other smaller river basins cross national boundaries. The dependency ratios of outside water flow range from 16 per cent in Jordan, 61 per cent in Iraq, 70 per cent in the Syrian Arab Republic and 93 per cent in Egypt.[63] For example, the 1999-2000 drought sparked conflict between the Syrian Arab Republic and Turkey over decreased water flows on the Tigris-Euphrates. The rainfall catchment area of the Tigris-Euphrates system lies primarily in Turkey, where it provides the Tigris with 51 per cent and the Euphrates with 89 per cent of their annual flow.[64] The 1999 drought resulted in reduced water flows into the Syrian Arab Republic, the downstream riparian, causing hydropower, irrigation and agricultural losses. Although groundwater aquifer recharge is largely internally generated, the increased occurrence of drought diminishes groundwater recharge, while increasing dependence on surface waters originating outside the region.

C. AGRICULTURAL VULNERABILITY

The agricultural sector is by far the most important water use activity in the region, with 86 per cent of all freshwater resources going to agriculture in 1997 (see table 3).[65] Agricultural water demand in 2000 ranged from 52 per cent in Kuwait to 95 per cent in the Syrian Arab Republic and Yemen. As the most water-dependent sector of the region, the agricultural sector and agricultural populations are therefore most susceptible to drought.

TABLE 3. SELECTED AGRICULTURAL STATISTICS ON THE ESCWA MEMBERS

ESCWA member	Value added in agriculture as a percentage of GDP (2002)	Agriculture water demand as a percentage of total demand (2000)	Irrigated lands as a percentage of croplands (2002)	Arable and permanent cropland/capita (2002)
Bahrain	-	57	66.6	0.01
Egypt	16.8	78	100.0	0.05
Iraq	-	92	57.8	0.25
Jordan	2.2	75	18.8	0.08
Kuwait	-	52	86.6	0.01
Lebanon	11.7	67	33.2	0.09
Oman	-	91	76.5	0.03
Qatar	-	72	61.9	0.04
Saudi Arabia	5.1	89	42.7	0.17
Syrian Arab Republic	23.5	95	24.6	0.32
United Arab Emirates	-	68	28.6	0.10
Palestinian territories	6.3	-	8.7	0.07
Yemen	15.2	95	30.0	0.08

Sources: FAO, FAOSTAT Statistical Databases, Rome, Food and Agriculture Organization of the United Nations, 2004; AQUASTAT Online Database, Rome, Food and Agriculture Organization of the United Nations, 2004; and World Bank, World Development Indicators Online Database, Washington, D.C., World Bank, 2004.

Agricultural sensitivity to drought depends on land use, intensity of agricultural activity, and soil moisture content. When demands on land and water resources exceed their sustainable levels, land degradation and desertification become an increasingly limiting factor for the land's productivity. In Western Asia, cropland per capita decreased from 0.33 ha per person in 1990 to 0.17 ha per person in 1996.[66]

---

[63] World Resources Institute, "EarthTrends Online Database", Washington, D.C., 2004.

[64] ESCWA, *Enhancing Negotiation Skills on International Water Issues in the ESCWA Region*, p. 9.

[65] Ibid., *Updating the Assessment of Water Resources in the ESCWA Member Countries*, p. 47.

[66] ICARDA, "Drought preparedness and mitigation of the effects of drought", paper presented at the Expert Group Meeting for the Preparation of the Sub-Regional Action Program on Combating Desertification and Drought in Western Asia, Muscat, Oman, September 1998, p. 1.

Agricultural stress on the natural resources of the region has exceeded the carrying capacity in many countries, with intensive agricultural pressure increasing land degradation and the region's vulnerability to drought, which in turn is evidenced by the increasing rate of desertification.

Arable cultivated lands comprise an estimated 76 per cent of the estimated total potential in the Middle East/North Africa region.[67] This figure indicates that most cultivable land is already being exploited and that there is limited scope for expansion. The aridity of the region means that irrigation is the principal means of agricultural intensification. Of the cultivated lands, 49.5 per cent were irrigated in the ESCWA region in 2002.[68] In non-irrigated areas, farms depend on the exploitation of shallow groundwater wells, and rainfall, making them more vulnerable to drought than irrigated farms. However, increased irrigation has depleted water resources and is likely to become an acute problem in the region. Therefore, although irrigation reduces dependence on rainfall, increased irrigation has reduced water resources to unsustainable levels in the region, depleting strategic reserves and thereby increasing water scarcity and vulnerability to drought.

Crop vulnerability to drought depends largely on climate, soil conditions, seed variety, drought-resistance of seed, timing of drought, temperatures and farming system. As such, crop vulnerability depends on local conditions, and thus assessments can only be made at the local level. However, certain crops are less able to adapt to higher temperatures and require more water, and therefore are more susceptible to drought. Examples include barley, wheat, chickpeas, lentils, olives, sunflowers and grapes.[69] Moreover, crops typically farmed in low rainfall areas with limited or no irrigation are generally more susceptible to drought. In the ESCWA region barley yields have been most adversely affected by drought.

At another level, low precipitation and drought results in zinc deficiencies in calcareous soils. This is particularly true of rain-fed areas in the ESCWA region, where zinc deficiency is widespread.[70] Zinc deficiency in soils results in reduction of grain yield and zinc concentration in the grain. Low zinc concentrations in plants and crops also decrease their nutritional status, thus affecting the health and nutritional status of communities dependent on these grains for food consumption. Drought exacerbates this problem further, thereby adversely impacting nutritional value and crop yields in these rain-fed areas.

Moreover, livestock resources contribute to 30 per cent of agricultural GDP in the Middle East region.[71] Livestock density in pastoral farming areas of the region exceeds the carrying capacity,[72] thereby increasing the vulnerability of pastures to drought. Reduced crop yields, dessicated water points, and increased costs of feed during drought years lead to the inability of livestock producers and pastoral farmers to maintain healthy stocks. The 1958-1962 drought in Jordan decimated 70 per cent of Jordan's camel herds, while the 1997 drought led to a 30 per cent reduction in Jordan's sheep flock because of disease, malnutrition or premature slaughter.[73] Livestock production, a significant component of agricultural production, is becoming increasingly vulnerable to drought, largely as a result of increased livestock stress on pastures and water resources.

---

[67] FAO and the World Bank, *Farming Systems and Poverty: Improving Farmers' Livelihoods in a Changing World*, table 3.1, "Major farming systems of the Middle East and North Africa" (2001).

[68] Ibid., FAOSTAT Online Database (Rome, 2004).

[69] E. DePauw, *An Agro-ecological Exploration of the Arabian Peninsula* (Aleppo [Syrian Arab Republic], ICARDA, 2002).

[70] M. Malakouti, "The role of zinc on the yield and grain fortification of wheat in the calcareous soils of dry lands", paper presented at the Seventh International Conference on Development of Drylands, held at Tehran, September 2003.

[71] P. Hazell and others, "Managing droughts in the low-rainfall areas of the Middle East and North Africa", International Food Policy Research Institute, Washington, D.C., September 2001, p. 4.

[72] FAO and the World Bank, *Farming Systems and Poverty: Improving Farmers' Livelihoods in a Changing World*, table 3.1.

[73] P. Hazell and others, "Managing droughts in the low-rainfall areas of the Middle East and North Africa", p. 7.

D. ENVIRONMENTAL VULNERABILITY

The desert terrain and unfavourable agro-ecological land constitutes about 63 per cent of the total area of the ESCWA region, and an increasing part of the permanent pasture areas is subject to erosion due to reduced vegetation cover.[74] This pressure on the land is being felt on a region where the land surface itself is fragile, often already degraded, and subject to high levels of natural erosion exacerbated by sand storms and drought. Land degradation, mostly in the form of desertification, is one of the region's most serious problems. Although desertification is often attributed to poor land use practices, drought deepens the effect and extends the area prone to desertification to encompass areas normally not at risk. Decreases in plant cover may also increase erosion, leading to a nearly irreversible loss of productive potential and subsequently to desertification. Therefore, desertification increases environmental vulnerability to drought, as less productive lands are available for economic livelihood, ecosystem biodiversity and food security.

Widespread deterioration of rangelands and increased desertification have resulted in loss of wildlife and their habitats, and of productive capacity of these lands. For example, in the period 1990-2000, many countries in the region witnessed a considerable drop in natural forest area, and crown cover of the remaining forest area remains sparse. Moreover, land-use patterns and poor agricultural practices have increased the rate of land degradation and the loss of arable lands. In Egypt, for example, about 32 per cent of the Nile Delta and 30 per cent of the Nile Valley are affected by salinity and water logging, lowering or eliminating their potential for crop production. In Iraq, salinity and water logging affect more than 50 per cent of the lower Rafadain Plain. In the Syrian Arab Republic, about 50 per cent of the irrigated land in the Euphrates Valley is seriously affected by salinity and water logging.[75] Poor land-use patterns coupled with drought have resulted in increased land degradation and desertification, further increasing the region's environmental vulnerability to drought.

Furthermore, intensive agricultural cropping and grazing reduces the amount of organic matter build-up, which feeds the soil after harvest. Low organic matter turnover reduces soil quality and increases its susceptibility to erosion. The loss of agricultural land is most acute in Jordan, Iraq, Lebanon, Syrian Arab Republic and Yemen, where fertile land is scarce and concentrated in the narrow coastal strip and river valleys. In Lebanon, land degradation is most acute on fragile steep lands exposed to extensive deforestation and soil erosion. Droughts increase the rate of degradation of lands, if the carrying capacity of the land is exceeded, and continued intensive land use during drought prevents recovery from periods of deficient rainfall.

As livestock production demand increases with population growth in the ESCWA region, grazing pressure on rangelands has increasingly become a much greater problem over the past two decades. Overgrazing reduces the productivity of rangelands and pasturelands over time, the protective groundcover and plant diversity and consequently the available nutritive value of the range plants. These changes in the soil increase its susceptibility to wind and water erosion, and thus enhance the vulnerability to drought.

Biodiversity in the ESCWA region is under increasing threat, partially due to human and drought-induced water resource losses. The depletion of groundwater levels on the western side of the Arabian Gulf is leading to the loss of a unique ecosystem of natural freshwater springs, affecting large numbers of plants and animals. This ecosystem was once widely distributed in the eastern province of Saudi Arabia and in Bahrain.[76] Human and drought-induced water depletion has significantly diminished the ecosystem area, threatening bird migration, indigenous plant and fish species.

---

[74] ESCWA, *Regional Report: Implementation of Agenda 21: Review of Progress Made since the United Nations Conference on Environment and Development, 1992* (Beirut, April 1997), p. 13.

[75] Ibid., p. 15.

[76] UNEP, "Global Environment Outlook –1", *Global State of the Environment Report 1997* (Nairobi, 1997).

E. SOCIO-ECONOMIC VULNERABILITY

The ESCWA members can be divided into three general categories: (a) the oil-dependent economies of Bahrain, Kuwait, Oman, Saudi Arabia, and United Arab Emirates; (b) the more diversified economies of the region, which include Egypt, Jordan, Lebanon, Syrian Arab Republic and Yemen; and (c) the conflict-stricken Iraq and Palestine. Of the 13 ESCWA members, only 3 do not export oil: Lebanon, Jordan and Palestine. The economies of the oil-dependent members have not diversified significantly beyond the petroleum industry, and their exports remain dominated by oil, with fuel exports in 2000 amounting to 63.8 per cent and 70 per cent of total exports in Bahrain and Kuwait respectively. The conflict-stricken ESCWA members have experienced conflict-induced limitations on economic growth and diversification, reaching unprecedented negative growth with the highest unemployment and poverty rates in the region, with significant segments of their populations dependent on humanitarian aid. These economies offer no resilience to an external shock such as drought. Furthermore, the ESCWA members with more diversified economies are still largely dependent on agriculture for employment of large sections of their labour forces and contribution to GDP. Although they have shown growth in manufacturing, commerce, transport, construction and other economic activities, labour market conditions and non-agricultural sector growth have not been able to keep up with labour force growth rates. Regional economic growth rates, estimated at 3.4 per cent for 1998-2003, cannot keep pace with regional annual labour force growth rates of 3.5 per cent for 1998-2003, nor absorb unemployment, estimated at 13.3 per cent in 2003 (table 4).[77]

TABLE 4. UNEMPLOYMENT, GDP GROWTH AND LABOUR FORCE
GROWTH IN THE MIDDLE EAST
(*Percentage*)

	2002	2003	1998-2003
GDP growth rate	3.3	4.7	3.4
Labour force growth rate	-	-	3.5
Unemployment	12.9	13.3	-
Youth unemployment	-	27.0	-

Source: International Labour Organization, *Global Employment Trends* (Geneva, 2004), p. 18.

The lack of economic diversification and employment generation in the non-agricultural sectors, continued dependence on the agricultural sector for employment of large segments of the population, and low economic growth compared with population and labour force growth further increase the region's vulnerability to drought. Overcoming the demographic pressures on employment, urbanization, land and water resources remains the region's largest challenge (table 5).

TABLE 5. POPULATION TRENDS IN THE ESCWA MEMBERS

ESCWA member	Population growth rate (2002-2015)	Fertility rate (Birth rate per woman) (2000-2005)	Population under 15 (2002)
Bahrain	1.8%	2.7	29.2%
Egypt	1.9%	3.3	35.2%
Iraq	2.6%	4.8	41.4%
Jordan	2.1%	3.6	38.0%
Kuwait	2.4%	2.7	26.1%
Lebanon	1.2%	2.2	29.6%
Oman	2.7%	5.0	37.2%
Qatar	1.3%	3.2	26.6%
Saudi Arabia	2.5%	4.5	39.1%
Syrian Arab Republic	2.2%	3.3	38.3%
United Arab Emirates	1.5%	2.8	25.8%
West Bank and Gaza Strip	3.3%	5.6	46.1%
Yemen	3.6%	7.0	48.7%

Source: UNDP Human Development Report Online Database, 2004.

---

[77] International Labour Organization, *Global Employment Trends* (Geneva, 2004), p. 18.

The population growth rate is exerting pressure on the region's already scarce water resources strained by both increasing domestic water requirements and agricultural sector demand for increased food production. The past two decades have witnessed population growth rates of between 2.5 and 3.5 per cent annually, with corresponding annual increases in water demand of 4 to 8 per cent.[78] The population pyramids of the countries in the region show up to half the population under the age of 15, translating into unabated pressure on the scarce water and land resources. Population growth has surpassed the water resources' sustainable carrying capacity in many countries in the region, and renewable water resources are buckling under the pressure, as evidenced by the deterioration of water quality in groundwater aquifers, the loss of valuable water resources, and ever-decreasing water per capita availability rates. Population growth generates increased demand for livestock and agricultural products, resulting in unprecedented pressure on arable and pasture lands. The high population growth rates of the region increase vulnerability to drought, as population pressure depletes water resources, and increased intensive agricultural cropping and grazing reduces land productivity.

High population growth is largely attributed to the high regional fertility rates, which although decreasing, continue to be high, with averages at 3.81 births per woman, well above the 2.9 averages for developing countries.[79] High fertility rates also translate into large household size, which in turn increases the households' economic vulnerability to poverty in case of a shock such as a drought.

While data on poverty in the ESCWA region are limited, drought and poverty create a scenario of misery and insecurity for millions of people, particularly in rural areas where employment is largely limited to agricultural activities and where poverty reduces household ability to recover from a drought. The United Nations Development Programme (UNDP) human poverty index, a composite index of several social and economic factors affecting poverty, reveals that poverty rates are high, particularly in Egypt, Iraq, Oman, and Yemen, where from 31 to 42 per cent of these countries' populations live in poverty. The 2001 Unified Arab Economic Report estimated that a little over half of the population in the Arab world lives below US$ 2 a day. Unemployment, a major contributor to poverty in the region, is high, with the labour force growth rate far outpacing growth of employment opportunities. The absence of adequate official social nets to protect the unemployed and the marginalized increases the vulnerability of the poor to external shocks such as drought (see table 6). As such, the rural poor are most vulnerable to drought.

TABLE 6. POVERTY AND UNEMPLOYMENT IN SELECTED ESCWA MEMBERS

ESCWA member	Human Poverty Index (2005)*	Population living under $2/day (1990-2000)*	Unemployment rate (Percentage in varying years)**
Bahrain	-	-	6.7[a]
Egypt	30.9%	43.9%	11.1[c]
Iraq	-	-	-
Jordan	8.1%	7.4%	18.8[c]
Kuwait	-	-	-
Lebanon	9.6%	-	-
Oman	21.1%	-	3.1[b]
Palestine	6.5%	-	-
Qatar	7.8%	-	-
Saudi Arabia	14.9%	-	-
Syrian Arab Republic	13.8%	-	8.1[b]
United Arab Emirates	-	-	2.6[c]
Yemen	40.3%	45.2%	13.5[a]

Sources: * UNDP Human Development Report Online Database, 2005, available at: http://hdr.undp.org/statistics/data/; and ** ESCWA, Application of Sustainable Development Indicators in the ESCWA Member Countries: Analysis of Results (E/ESCWA/ED/2000/4), p. 16.

a/ 1991; b/ 1993; c/ 1995.

[78] ESCWA, Updating the Assessment of Water Resources in the ESCWA Member Countries, p. 2.

[79] ESCWA, Where Do Arab Women Stand in the Development Process? A Gender-Based Statistical Analysis (2004), p. 3.

According to data compiled by the Sustainable Agricultural and Rural Development Team of ESCWA, 43 per cent of the populations in the region currently live in rural areas, depending largely on agriculture as a source of livelihood. Employment in the agricultural sector in the region is significant; however, employment figures disguise the actual employment levels or economic dependence on agriculture, as many children and women engage in unpaid agricultural employment.

The agricultural sector's contribution to GDP varies considerably from country to country in the region. The GCC members' (Bahrain, Kuwait, Oman, Qatar, Saudi Arabia and United Arab Emirates) average agricultural contribution to GDP is 10.1 per cent, while other agriculture-dependent ESCWA member countries recorded higher contributions to GDP: 16.8 per cent, 23.5 per cent, and 15.2 per cent in Egypt, the Syrian Arab Republic and Yemen respectively. In these more agriculture-dependent countries, the agricultural sector employs large percentages of the labour force: 33 per cent, 11 per cent, 32 per cent and 46 per cent in Egypt, Iraq, the Syrian Arab Republic and Yemen respectively.[80] The agricultural sector is able to absorb large portions of the region's labour force, as agriculture remains a largely labour-intensive activity. Other sectors of the economy tend to be less labour-intensive, and as such are unable to absorb significant amounts of labour. This is particularly true of the oil-producing industry, which is highly technical and mechanized. As such, drought, which affects the most water-dependent sector of the economy, also has an impact on large segments of the labour force. Past droughts in the region have resulted in significant agricultural livelihood and employment losses. The 1999 drought, experienced by many countries in the ESCWA region, resulted in cereal production losses in 1999 over 1998 of 88 per cent, 20 per cent, 40 per cent and 10 per cent in Jordan, Iraq, Syrian Arab Republic and Yemen respectively.[81] Small rivers and wadis dried up, affecting irrigated crops, while sheep farmers lost significant portions of their flocks. Landless households, the most vulnerable to drought, required food aid in Jordan and the Syrian Arab Republic. The rural populations of the region who have limited access to freshwater are most dependent on water for their economic livelihood, and are therefore among the most vulnerable to drought-related disasters.

According to FAO, agricultural communities have eight main categories of farming systems, based largely on climate and agro-ecological zones: irrigated; highland mixed; rain-fed mixed; dryland mixed; pastoral; sparse; coastal artisanal fishing; and urban.

TABLE 7. MAJOR FARMING SYSTEMS OF THE MIDDLE EAST AND NORTH AFRICA

Farming system	Land area (*Percentage of region*)	Agricultural population (*Percentage of region*)	Principal livelihoods	Prevalence of poverty
Irrigated	2	17	Fruits, vegetables, cash crops	Moderate
Highland mixed	7	30	Cereals, legumes, sheep, off-farm work	Extensive
Rain-fed mixed	2	18	Tree crops, cereals, legumes, off-farm work	Moderate (for small farmers)
Dryland mixed	4	14	Cereals, sheep, off-farm work	Extensive (for small farmers)
Pastoral	23	9	Sheep, goats, barley, off-farm work	Extensive (for small herders)
Sparse	62	5	Camels, sheep, off-farm work	Limited
Coastal artisanal fishing	1	1	Fishing, off-farm work	Moderate
Urban-based	1	6	Horticulture, poultry, off-farm work	Limited

Source: FAO, *Farming Systems and Poverty: Improving Farmers' Livelihoods in a Changing World*, table 3.1, "Major farming systems of Middle East and North Africa" (Rome).

---

[80] ESCWA, *Updating the Assessment of Water Resources in the ESCWA Member Countries*, p. 51.

[81] FAO, "Special Report: Drought Causes Extensive Crop Damage in the Near East, Raising Concerns for Food Supply Difficulty in Some Parts" (Rome, 16 July 1999), p. 3.

Table 7 shows the percentage of the Middle East and North Africa (MENA) region's[82] agricultural population engaged in the different farming system categories, and their corresponding principal livelihoods. From a socio-economic perspective, communities with lowered access to public services, low alternative employment opportunities, low household employment diversification, high dependence on rain-fed agriculture as a source of income, and high rates of poverty are especially vulnerable to drought. The table demonstrates that poverty, remoteness, and low livelihood diversification are more prevalent among marginal dry land, pastoral and small farmers. Poverty is conditioned by lack of access to the limited soil and water resources, by low productivity of marginal lands, by unpredictable rainfall, and also by low economic diversity of income.

A number of nomadic pastoral farmers move seasonally between low and high altitudes, or wetter zones and the dry steppes of the region. These communities living in dry areas with marginal land resources are among the poorest of rural communities and their livelihoods are affected by the risks inherent in dry land farming. With limited access to irrigation, dry land farmers depend largely on rainfall. Livestock also contribute to agricultural income and are a main source of family wealth for pastoral farmers. Livestock losses due to drought thus reduce pastoral farmers' wealth. For example, in the 1999 drought in the Syrian Arab Republic, herders in the Badia region lost large parts of their herds to disease, malnutrition and distress sales.[83] Without significant household income diversification, drought often translates into increased poverty for these communities. Socio-economic vulnerability to drought depends largely on household wealth and savings, availability of credit, household income diversity, farming systems, and access to public services.

A recent study by ICARDA, linking child nutrition and stunting to agricultural livelihoods in the Syrian Arab Republic, revealed that stunting was highest among barley and livestock farmers (25 per cent of the total population),[84] who are generally located in pastoral climates, and dependent on rainfall for agricultural production and on feed for livestock. Stunting was found to be lower among irrigated farming households (12.5 per cent of the total population), and lowest in urban households (1 per cent of total population).[85] This study reiterates the socio-economic and health vulnerability of dry land farming communities in drought-prone areas of the region.

While settlement patterns vary in the ESCWA region, populations are increasingly concentrated around urban areas and larger villages in rural areas. Domestic water demand has been rising as population, living standards, and urban migration increase and water delivery services expand. The urban population of the ESCWA region grew to 55.4 per cent of the total population in 1996, with 10 cities with populations above 1 million. Urban populations represent 31 per cent, 51 per cent, 70 per cent, 86 per cent, and 95 per cent of the total populations of Yemen, Syrian Arab Republic, Jordan, Lebanon and Kuwait respectively.[86] Domestic demand for water has been met by surface and groundwater, with the GCC countries depending significantly on desalinated water. Drought, although not widely felt by urban populations, adversely affects the long-term availability of water. Urban populations grow increasingly vulnerable to drought, and water shortages limit the availability of water per capita. Domestic per capita water consumption is already low, estimated (in litres per day per person) at 275 for Bahrain, 206 for Egypt, 345 for Iraq, 140 for Jordan, 219 for Lebanon, 495 for Qatar, 440 for Saudi Arabia, 118 for the Syrian Arab Republic, and 50 for Yemen,[87] and is fast descending to the "basic human water right" level of 180 m^3 per person per year, or 50 litres

---

[82] These figures cover the Middle East and North Africa (MENA), which includes Algeria, Bahrain, Djibouti, Egypt, Islamic Republic of Iran, Iraq, Israel, Jordan, Kuwait, Lebanon, Morocco, Oman, Qatar, Saudi Arabia, Syrian Arab Republic, Tunisia, United Arab Emirates, Yemen, and the West Bank and the Gaza Strip.

[83] FAO, "Drought conditions threaten food security of Syria's nomadic livestock producers" (Rome, Global Watch, Food and Agriculture Organization of the United Nations, 8 September 1999).

[84] ICARDA, "Poverty, Food Systems and Nutritional Well-Being of Children in Northwest Syria", ICARDA Development Seminar Series, Aleppo, 2005.

[85] Ibid.

[86] ESCWA, *Updating the Assessment of Water Resources in the ESCWA Member Countries*, p. 49.

[87] Ibid.

per person per day.[88] Drought induces water scarcity, which, in the absence of alternative water resources, results in reduced domestic consumption.

Already many major cities in the region practice water rationing, particularly during drought years. Rationing results in reduced sewage flows, increased pollutant concentrations, and deteriorating water quality, which can contribute to poor sanitation conditions and adverse health impacts. Poorer segments of the urban populations are most vulnerable as they are financially unable to supplement rationed water, and are thus more vulnerable to the adverse impacts of poor sanitation. Moreover, sewage conveyance systems have been unable to keep up with the rapid pace of urban growth in many cities in the region, resulting in poor sanitation in less affluent urban areas. For example, in Iraq and Yemen, 21 and 63 per cent of the respective populations do not have access to sanitation services.[89] In Oman, the Syrian Arab Republic and Yemen, 61 per cent, 20 per cent, and 31 per cent of these countries' respective total populations do not have access to safe water.[90]

The need for drought mitigation and preparedness planning is therefore critical, particularly for vulnerable pastoral and farming communities, and poorer urban populations. Water and land use patterns and policies of the ESCWA region are weakening resilience to drought, and increasing the risk and vulnerability to it. As such, sustainable resource management is the key to the success of drought management plans. The following section examines the level of drought preparedness and management at the regional level.

F. DROUGHT EARLY WARNING WITHIN THE ESCWA REGION

Within the ESCWA region, networks have been established to support capacity-building and information exchange among governments for developing drought early warning systems. The Network on Drought Management for the Near East, Mediterranean and Central Asia (NEMEDCA) was launched by FAO, ICARDA and CIHEAM in 2001 in an effort to contribute to the development and coordination of drought preparedness and mitigation plans and to promote the use of impact assessment tools. A Mediterranean Network on Management Strategies to Mitigate Drought is also being forged by CIHEAM and by the Mediterranean Agronomic Institute of Zaragoza (IAMZ). Furthermore, the United Nations International Strategy for Disaster Reduction and the International Drought Information Center (IDIC) have sought to work with the United Nations regional commissions to support drought preparedness efforts.

Arab countries are also assisted through the UNDP Trust Fund to Combat Desertification and Drought, which seeks to strengthen local capacities in dry land development and anti-desertification within the context of commitments made by Arab Member States under the United Nations Convention to Combat Desertification and Drought (UNCCDD). Saudi Arabia has implemented an information programme on the status of pastures, aimed at livestock breeders and based on drought monitoring, with the goal of facilitating livestock mobility and promoting the livelihood of herders.

The national agricultural research systems (NARS) in ESCWA member States have acquired, to varying degrees, meteorological databases, remote sensing equipment, computers, and information systems to monitor climate and drought occurrence.[91] However, these technologies and equipment are not fully utilized to forecast drought, nor provide information to drought-prone communities and farmers. As such, national-level drought early warning systems are virtually non-effective in the ESCWA region. Moreover, the region has an overwhelming need for socio-economic drought early warning systems. The key challenges to establishing comprehensive, multidisciplinary socio-economic drought early warning systems in the region are outlined below.

---

[88] ESCWA, *Enhancing Negotiation Skills on International Water Issues in the ESCWA Region*, p. 5.

[89] UNDP Human Development Report Online Database, 2004.

[90] Ibid.

[91] ICARDA, "The West Asian Joint Program for Drought Preparedness and Mitigation of the Effects of Drought, Sub-Regional Program on Combating Desertification and Drought in Western Asia" (Aleppo, November 1998), p. 6.

1. *Institutional capacity*

Institutional arrangements and inter-agency communication and information exchange are crucial to the success of an early warning system. This is especially true of a socio-economic drought early warning system, which is multidisciplinary and multi-tiered by nature. As such, data must be coordinated at the local, district and national levels as well as across responsible institutions. Currently, the countries in the region do not have socio-economic drought monitoring focal points or institutions that could act as central coordination units for data analysis and information dissemination. Drought vulnerability assessments are not conducted, nor are any early warning bulletins issued.[92] In the ESCWA region, there is therefore a need for the creation of drought management units with a clear mandate, authority, and multidisciplinary staff.

The prevailing systems for decision-making in many ESCWA countries tend to separate economic, technological, social, and environmental factors at the policy, planning, and management levels. In order to establish a drought early warning system, decision-making must therefore be adjusted to accord priority to integrating environmental, meteorological, agricultural, social and economic information in policy and planning. Significant changes in the institutional structures will be needed to enable a more integrated approach, especially in drought-vulnerable economic sectors and communities.

Furthermore, transparent partnerships across institutions for the operation of effective multidisciplinary early warning systems are generally lacking. Meteorological data networks, including those independent of national meteorological services, do not share information. In many cases, meteorological and other data are provided at prohibitive costs, while agricultural research institutions do not share their local expertise in agricultural applications.[93] Therefore, there is a need for meteorological services to form partnerships to assist each other with data collection, data pooling, and data sharing in the ESCWA region.

2. *Technical capacity and monitoring*

In any drought monitoring system, meteorological services play a key role. In the northern ESCWA region, meteorological networks are well established, well sited in terms of representation of differing agro-ecological and climatic zones, and adequately operational.[94] However, in the Arabian Peninsula, basic data are lacking since the number of meteorological stations are inadequate, given the size of the Peninsula and the large variations in agro-climatic conditions.[95]

In the ESCWA region in general, there is a lack of analytical tools for drought monitoring, of suitable information products and of information-sharing. For example, although efforts have been made to develop suitable drought indicators, well-established drought indicators such as the Percent of Normal, Standardized Precipitation Index, Palmer Drought Severity Index, and Deciles are generally not used.[96] In addition, weather parameters such as temperature, sunshine and humidity, which are necessary for measuring the extent of drought, are insufficient given the diverse landscapes, topographies and temperature regimes within the ESCWA region. The costs associated with information-sharing make the data collection process expensive.

3. *Financial capacity*

The cost of establishing effective early warning systems is high, since the tools needed include remote sensing, high-resolution imagery and expensive modelling tools. For example, early warning systems for crop yield and production forecasting used by FAO and the European Union are based on sophisticated crop yield models based on crop-specific data, growth simulations and production trend functions using remote

---

[92] E. DePauw, "Drought Early Warning Systems in West Asia and North Africa".

[93] Ibid.

[94] Ibid.

[95] E. DePauw, *An Agro-ecological Exploration of the Arabian Peninsula*, p. 65.

[96] Ibid., "Drought Early Warning Systems in West Asia and North Africa".

sensing and GIS.[97] The regular data requirements of these systems make them very expensive to operate and maintain. Therefore, one of the major impediments to drought planning is its cost. Policy makers may find it difficult to justify the costs of a plan, and its associated technical tools, institutions and expenses, which are immediate and fixed, against the unknown costs of some future drought. In a region where many nations' government spending is stretched to fill pressing development needs, finding adequate resources to launch and operate a drought early warning system is challenging. However, the even higher cost of drought disaster emergency response emphasizes the necessity of developing strategies to mitigate future drought occurrences, particularly in a region that is water-scarce and arid, and where climate change threatens to increase the incidence and severity of drought in the future.

---

[97] Ibid.

V. JORDAN

From 1995 to 2001, Jordan endured mild to severe drought conditions. The 1998/99 agricultural season, one of the driest winters on record in Jordan, led to a sharp drop in dam water levels, seriously reducing agricultural production and exacerbating the economic problems facing the country. Rainfall in 1999 dropped by as much as 70 per cent in some zones of the country, leaving agricultural yields and production the worst recorded in the past four decades.[98] This, in turn, had serious repercussions on the rural populations dependent on the agricultural sector; as incomes fell sharply, assets were liquidated, and livestock herds were lost to disease, malnutrition, premature slaughter and distress sales. The Jordanian economy, squeezed by the United Nations trade embargo on Iraq, the loss of markets in the Gulf States, and regional political conflicts, was unable adequately to absorb the shock of drought. Limited off-farm economic opportunities and high rates of unemployment reduced the economy's capacity to absorb rural-urban labour migration. Moreover, the 1999 fall in foreign currency revenues and heavy foreign debt repayments limited Jordan's capacity to import the shortfall in agricultural production. The state of the economy and the scale and severity of the drought limited the Government's ability to mitigate its effects. The following section summarizes the climatic, water resource, agricultural, environmental, and socio-economic characteristics of Jordan that increase its vulnerability to drought.

A. CLIMATIC VULNERABILITY

Jordan, covering a land area of about 89,200 square kilometres (km^2), of which arable land is less than 5 per cent, has a climate that is characterized by hot, dry summers and cool, wet winters.[99] Jordan can be divided into five agro-ecological zones (figure IV):[100]

(a) *The Badia* (semi-desert zone): This zone covers 90 per cent of the country and is characterized by a very sparse vegetation cover, with annual rainfall less than 200 millimetres (mm). In the past it was only used for grazing; however, in the last two decades, 20,000 ha have been irrigated, using groundwater to grow vegetables, fruit trees and cereals, especially barley;

(b) *Marginal arid zone*: This zone comprises the plains between the Badia (semi-desert) and the Highlands, receiving 200-250 mm annual rainfall. Rain-fed crops are mainly barley, yielding 300-700 kilograms (kg) per ha. The estimated production of the arid zone is 60,000 tons of barley grain, 80,000 tons of straw, and 10,000 tons of dry fodder barley. Sheep and goats graze around the cultivated areas;

(c) *Semi-arid zone*: The Highlands, which are a succession of catchments and sub-catchments with varying topography, receive 350-500 mm annual rainfall. Low sloping areas are cultivated with wheat and summer vegetables, while intermediate sloping areas are cultivated with tree crops, especially olives. Mountainous areas are used for grazing, forestry and fruit trees. The estimated forage production of the mountainous grazing in this zone is about 13,500 tons of dry matter;

(d) *Semi-humid zone*: A small area of the Highlands, the semi-humid zone, receives over 500 mm annual rainfall. Wheat cultivation is dominant on flat areas, olive and fruit trees are cultivated on land with slope ranges between 9 and 25 per cent, while forest trees are dominant in areas with slopes over 25 per cent. The area of forest is about 40,000 ha, and the estimated forage production is about 12,000 tons;

(e) *The Ghor zone* (the Rift Valley): The Ghor is the most important zone for vegetable, citrus and banana production, because of its tropical climate and the availability of irrigation water. The Jordan Valley and the southern Ghor are among the most important agricultural areas, as there is a permanent source of water from the Yarmouk River, side dams and surface water.

---

[98] FAO, "Worst drought in decades decimates cereal crops in Jordan" (Rome, Global Watch, Food and Agriculture Organization of the United Nations, 3 June 1999).

[99] Ibid., "Country Pasture/Forage Resource Profiles: Jordan" (Rome, Food and Agriculture Organization of the United Nations, 2001), p. 1.

[100] Ibid.

Figure IV. Vegetation and precipitation zones of Jordan

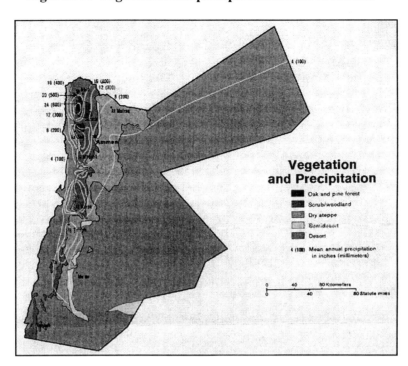

Source: "Jordan – Vegetation and Precipitation", Jordan Maps, Perry-Castañeda Library Map Collection, University of Texas at Austin, 1978. Available at: http://www.lib.utexas.edu/maps/jordan.html.

Over 90 per cent of the country receives less than 200 mm precipitation per year, and variations in precipitation and temperature are high, making Jordan climatically vulnerable to drought. The 1998 winter recorded the lowest rainfall on record; the rains were two months late, poorly distributed and finished early.

Both surface and groundwater entering and in Jordan are highly dependent on rainfall, with the total quantity of rainfall estimated to be 8,425 million m^3 per year on average. Of this rainfall, 92.2 per cent evaporates, 5.4 per cent goes to the recharge of underground aquifers, and 2.4 per cent runs off as surface water. Any variation in rainfall or temperature therefore increases vulnerability to drought.[101] Micro-climatic changes over the last 70 years, due to climate change, human-induced land degradation, and desertification, have resulted in a recorded annual decline in precipitation of 0.7-1.8 mm.[102] This trend will only intensify Jordan's climatic vulnerability to drought.

B. WATER RESOURCE VULNERABILITY

Jordan is one of the most water-scarce countries in the world, with annual freshwater per capita at 168 m^3 in 1997,[103] well below the critical water scarcity level of 500 m^3 per person per year. Jordan's high population growth has placed increasing pressure on its scarce water resources, and current water demand trends and the unsustainable use of renewable water resources threaten the viability and water quality in groundwater aquifers. Jordan's WUSI is measured at 118 per cent, revealing water withdrawals beyond replenishment levels. Unlike the GCC member States, Jordan does not currently possess the financial resources for desalination, and opportunities for large captures of new water are few and costly, both in terms

[101] A. de Sherbinin and V. Dompka, eds., "Case Study: Jordan, Population Dynamics in Arid Regions: The Experience of the Azraq Oasis Conservation Project", by F. Fariz and A. Hatough-Bouran, in *Water and Population Dynamics: Case Studies and Policy Implications* (American Association for the Advancement of Science, 1998).

[102] Interview with Abdel Nabi Fardous, Director General, National Center for Agricultural Research and Technology Transfer, Amman, 22 March 2005.

[103] ESCWA, *Application of Sustainable Development Indicators in the ESCWA Member Countries: Analysis of Results*, p. 22.

of withdrawal and transport to demand centres.[104] Drought exacerbates Jordan's water resource vulnerability by diminishing water replenishment rates and thereby reducing the annual renewable water resources available. In 1999, rainfall dropped to about 30 per cent of its annual average,[105] while in 2000, rainfall reached only 56 per cent of its annual average, leaving Jordan's six dams only 33 per cent full.[106]

According to the Ministry of Water and Irrigation, safe production levels of the shallow renewable aquifers are estimated to be 275 million m^3 per year.[107] However, skewed water pricing and years of unlimited issuance of water well licences have resulted in its over-exploitation, and many aquifers go out of production every year because of a decline in the quality and quantity of their waters. In the eastern desert regions, such as Duliel and Azraq, over-pumping from deep aquifers in the 1980s and 1990s resulted in a tenfold increase in water salinity, and soils in these places have degraded to the point of unsuitability for cultivation.[108] Irrigation and domestic water conveyance losses are significant too. According to the Ministry of Water and Irrigation, unaccounted for water in Amman has recently reached a level of 43 per cent.[109] Water scarcity, population pressures and the lack of cohesive water resource management amplifies Jordan's water resource vulnerability to drought.

For much of its surface water, Jordan is dependent on major rivers, the Yarmouk and the Jordan, and the country relies on the Jordan River Basin's surface waters for more than half of its water consumption.[110] However, these rivers originate outside Jordan's political boundaries, and as Jordan is a downstream riparian country with regard to the Jordan River Basin, it remains in a difficult position as regards this politically-charged basin. Agricultural return flows and untreated wastewaters of upper riparian countries are the sources of pollution to the lower Jordan River. Rainwater contributes the majority of the water in the Jordan River Basin, collected for the most part in the upper basin, north of Lake Tiberias. With a dependency ratio of 16 per cent on surface water from outside the country, and as a downstream riparian country, Jordan's water supply is extremely vulnerable to the conflicts in the region. Threats posed by cyclical drought compound water scarcity and increase international competition and conflict over shared water resources, in one of the most water-scarce river basins in the world. The 1999-2001 drought caused conflict over water flows between Jordan and Israel, its riparian neighbour on the Jordan River, and between Jordan and the Syrian Arab Republic, its riparian neighbour on the Yarmouk River. In July of 2000, Jordanian and Syrian water officials negotiated for some 60,000 m^3 to be pumped daily for two months, to accommodate Jordan's drought-induced water crisis.[111] Although Jordan's groundwater aquifer recharge is largely internally generated, the increased occurrence of drought diminishes groundwater recharge, while increasing dependence on surface waters originating outside the country.

C. AGRICULTURAL VULNERABILITY

The agricultural sector utilizes 75 per cent of Jordan's total water withdrawals annually and is therefore most water-dependent and most vulnerable to drought. Recent droughts have affected all crops and farming systems. Agricultural production dropped, from 1997/98 to 1998/99, by 33 per cent for vegetables, 73 per cent for olives, 34 per cent for grapes, and 30 per cent for other fruit trees.[112] The drought reduced

---

[104] Interview with Fayez Bataineh, Ministry of Water and Irrigation, Amman, 21 March 2005.

[105] FAO, "Worst drought in decades decimates cereal crops in Jordan".

[106] "Jordan announces summer water rationing plan for parched kingdom", Associated Press, 26 April 2000.

[107] Interview with Fayez Bataineh, Ministry of Water and Irrigation, Amman, 21 March 2005.

[108] F. Fariz and A. Hatough-Bouran, Case Study: Jordan, Population Dynamics in Arid Regions: The Experience of the Azraq Oasis Conservation Project, p. 6.

[109] Interview with Fayez Bataineh, Ministry of Water and Irrigation, Amman, 21 March 2005.

[110] ESCWA, *Enhancing Negotiation Skills on International Water Issues in the ESCWA Region.*

[111] "Syria pumps water to Jordan to alleviate drought", Associated Press, 13 August 2000.

[112] FAO, "FAO/WFP Crop and Food Supply Assessment Mission to the Kingdom of Jordan" (Rome, Food and Agriculture Organization of the United Nations, 26 May 1999), p. 12.

wheat and barley production in 1999 by 88 per cent.[113] On average, wheat and barley provide 10 per cent of domestic requirements,[114] but in 1999 production met only 0.6 per cent of domestic demand.[115]

Jordan's arable land, amounting to 400,000 ha or 5 per cent of the total area, is concentrated in the northwest-central areas (Jordan Valley and Highlands). Of this land, 18.8 per cent is irrigated. In the Jordan Valley, water from the Yarmouk and Zarqa rivers and smaller wadis is distributed to farm tanks. Highland irrigation is provided from pump boreholes and springs that are used for full time and supplementary irrigation of vegetables and fruit trees and account for 60 per cent of the national production.[116] The remaining agricultural areas, amounting to 80 per cent of the cultivated area, are rain-fed.[117] As such, the agricultural sector is highly rain-dependent and characterized by unstable production due to erratic rainfall and regular drought. For example, cereals are produced under rain-fed conditions during winter, with annual production varying depending on rainfall. In 1986, a drought year, Jordan produced 22,000 tons of wheat, down from 63,000 tons in 1985, but produced 130,000 tons in 1987 when the rains returned.[118]

Remote sensing data show that declines in food production during the 1999 drought were most severe in the most agriculturally productive zones, namely the Highlands and the Jordan Valley. Vast areas of cultivated but non-productive land are apparent in every Governorate. Chart 1 below shows rainfall in the 1998/99 winter against average rainfall received at monitoring stations in the Jordan Valley and the Highlands.

Chart 1. 1998/99 Jordan Valley and Highland monthly rainfall

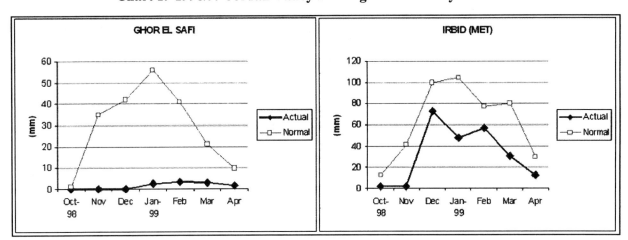

Rain-fed and irrigated fruit and vegetable production was severely reduced in 1999. Crop yields dropped from 200-400 kg/ha in non-drought years to 0-50 kg/ha during the drought.[119] For almost all rain-fed cereal farmers, the investment in cultivation and sowing at around US$ 45-57 per ha was lost, except where the failed crops had been sold to herders for grazing at prices ranging from US$ 15-45 per ha.[120]

---

[113] UNEP, "Disasters: West Asia: Drought", Global Environment Outlook 3 (Nairobi, 2002).

[114] FAO, "Worst drought in decades decimates cereal crops in Jordan".

[115] FAO, "FAO/WFP Crop and Food Supply Assessment Mission to the Kingdom of Jordan", p. 2.

[116] Ibid., p. 4.

[117] FAO, "Country Pasture/Forage Resource Profiles: Jordan", p. 3.

[118] R. Rinehart and others, "Agriculture", in Jordan: A Country Study, Country Studies Series, U.S. Government Printing Office, 1980.

[119] Interview with Abdel Nabi Fardous, Director General, National Center for Agricultural Research and Technology Transfer, Amman, Jordan, 22 March 2005.

[120] FAO, "FAO/WFP Crop and Food Supply Assessment Mission to the Kingdom of Jordan", p. 8.

Equally drought-impacted was the Badia region, where most of Jordan's herders and sheep stocks are located and where Badia vegetation is a significant source of feed. Sheep and goat systems produce about 20 per cent of domestic milk and 24 per cent of domestic red meat, and are more vulnerable to drought as the use of home-grown cereals, cereal by-products and range grazing dominates the feed composition.[121] Rangeland barley and wheat bran are fed up to nine months per year.[122] The failure of the Badia rangelands and most mountain pastures to produce edible biomass during the spring of 1999, and the decline in cereal production and crop residues in the Highlands and Jordan Valley, resulted in a lack of feed for livestock, and widespread under-nutrition and disease in the sheep population; the incidence of foot and mouth disease increased and lamb mortality rates increased by 5-15 per cent.[123] Although the Jordanian Government reintroduced subsidies for cereal feed, the costs of feed and water were significantly higher than in non-drought years, to the extent that most flock owners suffered financial losses. The overall effect of the drought was that the Jordanian agricultural industry was, and continues to be, under severe threat.

D. ENVIRONMENTAL VULNERABILITY

Land degradation, mostly in the form of desertification, is one of the country's most serious problems. Although desertification is often attributed to poor land use practices, drought deepens the effect and extends the area prone to desertification to encompass areas normally not at risk. There has been a recorded decline in vegetation cover and increased desertification of over 80 per cent of Jordan's land area,[124] owing primarily to increased agricultural pressure and water use for non-ecological purposes. Decreases in plant cover due to drought increase erosion and lead to a nearly irreversible loss of productive potential, and subsequently to desertification. This has resulted in micro-climate changes, as soil emission of radiation is higher on bare soil, which in turn has caused a recorded decline in rainfall received and in higher temperatures, permanently changing the climate of those areas, and shrinking or eliminating habitats for significant species.[125] Scientific analysis of climate change reveals that a 2°C temperature increase can produce a 20 per cent decrease in precipitation.[126]

One example of habitat loss is the Azraq Oasis in the middle of the Jordanian Badia, a natural habitat for numerous aquatic and terrestrial species, and migratory birds. Increasing incidence of drought and environmentally damaging activities dried out much of the Oasis, which supports 209 species of birds and 133 kinds of vascular plants, seven of which are unique to Azraq.[127] The Oasis, although a national reserve and Ramsar site, remains threatened by drought and water scarcity.[128] Azraq's aquifers supply Amman with 25 per cent of its water.[129] Unsustainable use of this water, particularly in drought years, threatens not only to lower water tables, but also to diminish water quality through infiltration of brackish water because of over-pumping. This greatly increases the vulnerability of the oasis and its wildlife.

---

[121] Ibid., p. 4.

[122] Ibid., p. 5.

[123] Ibid., p. 13.

[124] Interview with Abdel Nabi Fardous, Director General, National Center for Agricultural Research and Technology Transfer, Amman, Jordan, 22 March 2005.

[125] Ibid.

[126] Intergovernmental Panel on Climate Change, *IPCC Special Report on The Regional Impacts of Climate Change: An Assessment of Vulnerability*, chap. 7, "Middle East and Arid Asia" (Geneva, 2000).

[127] F. Fariz and A. Hatough-Bouran, Case Study: Jordan, Population Dynamics in Arid Regions: The Experience of the Azraq Oasis Conservation Project, p. 12.

[128] The Ramsar Convention on Wetland, available at: http://www.ramsar.org.

[129] Interview with Fayez Bataineh, Ministry of Water and Irrigation, Amman, Jordan, March 21, 2005.

Overgrazing in the Badia in particular has also exacerbated environmental vulnerability to drought, causing the destabilization of soil structures and the loss of many soil-fixing organic materials. This damage makes these lands more vulnerable to other forces of erosion, such as run-off, wind and drought.[130]

E. SOCIO-ECONOMIC VULNERABILITY

Jordan, with its limited natural resource base and domestic market, has been largely dependent on external trade and foreign income inflows for economic development. Inflows of foreign aid and remittances from expatriates have permitted domestic consumption to outpace production, causing gross national product (GNP) to exceed GDP. Jordan's economic growth and contraction to a large degree has mirrored the booms, busts and conflicts of the region. In the wake of the first Gulf war in 1991 and the subsequent trade embargo on Iraq, the loss of the markets of Iraq and the Gulf States and suppressed overall economic investment revealed Jordan's vulnerability to external forces. Although recent economic developments, such as the signing of several free trade agreements and Jordan's entry into the WTO, are aimed at increasing economic diversity, the country remains highly vulnerable to external shocks, including drought. The 1999 drought, for example, came at a time where the economy was already strained by the loss of regional markets, experiencing high unemployment, and holding low foreign currency reserves. Rural-urban migration placed increasing strain on the economy, which already could not absorb the high rate of unemployment (unofficially estimated at 25 per cent in 1999), while a fall in foreign currency revenues and debt repayment of US$ 850 million per year constrained Jordan's capacity to increase imports.[131] Government efforts could not adequately mitigate the significant financial losses, increased poverty and subsequent rural-urban migration.

Like other countries in the ESCWA region, Jordan continues to have a high population growth rate, fuelled by its fertility rate of 3.6 children per woman during her reproductive years. Although population growth is projected to slow to 2.1 per cent between 2002 and 2015, it has placed increasingly high pressure on Jordan's scarce natural resources, particularly water and arable land, which is already low at 0.08 ha/capita. This has in turn greatly decreased the country's food security, as the food import bill increases with population growth.

The agricultural sector's contribution to GDP has diminished over the years from almost 40 per cent in the 1950s[132] to about 2 per cent currently, in part owing to water scarcity and the impacts of historic droughts, in addition to the growth of other sectors of the economy and the loss of traditional agricultural export markets. In spite of the agriculture sector's low contribution to GDP, in its socio-economic dimensions, it is still a fundamental sector of the national economy. Agriculture is the main income source of about 15 to 20 per cent of the population, employs about 6 per cent of the workforce,[133] is a generator of activities in the other economic sub-sectors, and plays a central role in food security and trade balance improvement.

The drought affected all crops and farming systems. While irrigation provided a buffer against more significant losses, access to surface irrigation water was cut, both by diminished availability and Government rationing. Farming losses were not only recorded in yield losses; input costs for farmers were increased owing to shortage and increased demand. For example, for almost all rain-fed cereal farmers the cost of cultivation and sowing (at around 30 to 40 Jordanian dinars (JD) per ha) was lost, except where the failed crops were sold for grazing (at around JD 10 to JD 30 per ha).[134] Minor field crops of lentils and chickpeas, normally producing from 4,000 to 5,000 tons of grain, were eaten green,[135] and many farmers were forced to

---

[130] F. Fariz and A. Hatough-Bouran, Case Study: Jordan, Population Dynamics in Arid Region: The Experience of the Azraq Oasis Conservation Project, p. 14.

[131] FAO, "FAO/WFP Crop and Food Supply Assessment Mission to the Kingdom of Jordan", p. 2.

[132] R. Rinehart and others, "Agriculture", in Jordan: A Country Study.

[133] FAO, "Country Pasture/Forage Resource Profiles: Jordan", p. 3.

[134] FAO, "FAO/WFP Crop and Food Supply Assessment Mission to the Kingdom of Jordan", p. 8.

[135] Ibid.

leave their fields fallow for lack of water and finances. To assist, the Government instituted a farming subsidy programme in the Jordan Valley, whereby fallow lands were "rented" from farmers, in an effort to mitigate the impact of the drought and to conserve scarce water.

Despite the sale of failed crops and crop residues to herders, the lack of feed, due to decreased rangeland vegetation and barley production, became an acute problem for all herders, particularly those of the Badia. The drought virtually wiped out rangeland vegetation, leaving many livestock herders facing bankruptcy and small farmers without income and with an increasing debt. In the Badia, the drought-induced failure of rangeland to produce edible vegetation resulted in an increase in cereal use for feed, at a significantly higher cost to herders. Government reintroduction of subsidies for cereal feed reduced prices to JD 75/ton for barley and JD 65/ton for wheat bran.[136] Although the subsidies were helpful, farmers who were unable to raise credit to purchase feed experienced lower levels of production and higher levels of livestock disease and malnutrition. Most coped by selling slaughter stock at lower weights and prices, as livestock prices dropped due to premature selling.[137] Smaller herders faced bankruptcy and left the Badia to seek employment in urban areas, but, in general, jobs were difficult to find, as reflected by the high rate of unemployment. This increased rural-urban migration during drought placed pressure on urban areas and services, as well as on the Government's ability to provide social services, resulting in increasing levels of urban poverty and unemployment. Lower crop yields due to drought translated into higher food prices in urban markets, leading to higher food expenditure at a time of economic recession.

Following three of the driest winters on record, dam water levels reached an unprecedented low in 1999 and 2001, reaching as low as 3 per cent of the country's eight main reservoirs.[138] Water scarcity is critical in Jordan, where the average share of water per capita is 156 litres per day for all consumption purposes.[139] Jordan is the only country in the region rationing year-round owing to shortages. Households receive, on average, 80 litres per day, delivered only one day (12-24 hours) a week under a rationing system instituted 36 years ago.[140] Although public piped water supplies reach 95 per cent of the population, the quality of water supply suffers from interruptions, increased pollutant concentrations, and cross-contamination, which constitute a serious threat to public health.[141]

FAO estimated that about one quarter of the Jordanian population was strongly affected by the 1999 drought, experiencing complete loss of income, indebtedness and destitution. Small farmers sold assets to pay debts and landless labourers found themselves jobless with no alternative job opportunities. Smallholders who had lost their harvests and inputs, small-scale herders and landless rural households were most vulnerable and hardest hit. In 1999, FAO instituted an emergency food assistance programme to serve 180,000 of those hardest hit. Although the assistance programme, in combination with Government measures, did mitigate the impacts of the drought, the response was more ad hoc and reactive than preventative.

F. DROUGHT EARLY WARNING AND MITIGATION IN JORDAN

The Government officially declared a state of drought emergency in January 1999 and introduced a range of measures to save water and to support the struggling farming population,[142] including:[143]

---

[136] Ibid., p. 6.

[137] Ibid.

[138] "Water shortages plague Jordan", US Water News Online, September 2002.

[139] World Health Organization, *Country Cooperation Strategy for WHO and Jordan, 2003-2007* (Cairo, WHO Regional Office for the Eastern Mediterranean, 2003), p. 6.

[140] "Jordan facing water shortage", US Water News Online, July 1998.

[141] "Water shortages plague Jordan", p. 6.

[142] FAO, "FAO/WFP Crop and Food Supply Assessment Mission to the Kingdom of Jordan".

[143] Ibid.

(a) Reducing the price of barley and wheat bran, from JD 85 to JD 65/ton and from JD 95 to JD 75/ton;

(b) Providing free water service to flocks;

(c) Rescheduling loans from the Agricultural Credit Corporation (ACC);

(d) Renting land from Jordan Valley farmers to keep it fallow and prevent rural-urban migration;[144]

(e) Restricting irrigation water to 30 per cent[145] to the Jordan Valley and 50 per cent[146] to tree crops in the Highlands.

Although valid and valuable, these emergency measures did not fully mitigate the impact of the drought. Government response to drought has been reactionary as no early warning system or national drought preparedness plan has been established. The seriousness of the 1999-2001 drought and the increasing incidence of drought emphasize the necessity of developing strategies to mitigate future droughts and their impacts. To that effect, Jordan's National Center for Agricultural Research and Technology Transfer (NCARTT) has begun to develop a drought monitoring strategy. This strategy includes the development of a drought-monitoring unit reporting to the Prime Ministry, relying on drought data from a network of 291 weather stations and established agricultural research stations across the country, and supplemented by the GIS facilities of NCARTT.[147] Until such an institution is in place and operating, the Government continues to address drought and its impacts in an ad hoc and segmented manner, in the face of the following key challenges to establishing a drought preparedness plan.

1. *Institutional capacity*

Currently, three ministries are involved in water supply, management and use: the Ministries of Agriculture, Environment, and Water and Irrigation. NCARTT is involved in drought monitoring, under which integrated water resource management, management information systems (MIS) for crop water requirements, Badia projects, and other related projects would be unified. In general, Jordan has adequate data-collecting institutions for drought monitoring; however, the current response to drought is not institutionalized and has been ad hoc and crisis-oriented without adequate information exchange and coordination. Drought vulnerability assessments are not conducted, nor are any early warning bulletins issued.

Water demand management, as a component of a drought mitigation strategy, remains a challenge in Jordan. Although the Ministry of Water and Irrigation has undertaken several steps to improve water management and use in the country, such as increased water conservation awareness, increased use of water-saving technology, replacement of water conveyance pipes, increased use of treated wastewater in agriculture, and a ban on new well licensing, water demand management through water pricing has largely not been instituted in Jordan, particularly in the agricultural sector. Supply of water in Jordan is considered a right by the public, and any manipulation of water demand through pricing is viewed as highly political. Farmers with well licences pump water at no cost, beyond sustainable and allowable levels, resulting in over-pumping of groundwater, a drop in water table levels, and a decrease in water quality due to infiltration of brackish water. Although recent attempts to regulate water use and pricing, particularly for private wells, have raised the price, integrated water resources management remains a challenge for the Jordanian Government since significant changes in the institutional structures would be necessary to enable a more multidisciplinary and integrated approach to drought monitoring and early warning.

---

[144] Interview with Fayez Bataineh, Ministry of Water and Irrigation, Amman, Jordan, 21 March 2005.

[145] FAO, "FAO/WFP Crop and Food Supply Assessment Mission to the Kingdom of Jordan".

[146] Interview with Fayez Bataineh, Ministry of Water and Irrigation, Amman, Jordan, 21 March 2005.

[147] Interview with Safa' Mazaher, GIS Lab Administrator, National Center for Agricultural Research and Technology Transfer, Amman, Jordan, 22 March 2005.

2. *Technical capacity and monitoring*

In any drought monitoring system, meteorological services play a key role. Jordan's weather stations are numerous and well distributed across the country. Data from these weather stations and agricultural research stations are also centrally collected and disseminated within NCARTT, which also possesses the analytical tools for drought monitoring, including strong GIS capacity. However, data on drought are segmented (usually by geographic region), and not uniform countrywide. In addition, there is to date no baseline study for drought.[148] Information on drought is not integrated, and there is no umbrella institution for drought response.[149] Although a good level of information-sharing occurs, it is still not at a level to support a coordinated drought mitigation strategy across institutions and responsible ministries.

---

[148] Interview with Abdel Nabi Fardous, Director-General, National Center for Agricultural Research and Technology Transfer, Amman, Jordan, 22 March 2005.

[149] Ibid.

VI. THE SYRIAN ARAB REPUBLIC

As part of a wider regional drought affecting the ESCWA region, the 1999-2001 drought was the worst in four decades, seriously affecting crop and livestock production in the Syrian Arab Republic, with serious repercussions on the food security of a large segment of the population as incomes fell sharply, particularly among the rural small farmers and herders. Urban populations, particularly in the southern part of the Syrian Arab Republic, experienced water shortages. Owing to a decrease in the flow of the Euphrates River, irrigation canals dried up and hydro-powered electricity plants were unable to operate at capacity. Economic growth was affected as agricultural production fell sharply, reducing the contribution of agricultural income to GDP. Although the Government made extensive efforts to reduce the effects of the drought, especially on herders, by providing extra resources, feed rations, water and veterinary supplies, they were inadequate given the drought's scale and severity. The drought coincided with an economic slowdown caused by the fall in oil prices, which reduced the country's resilience to drought and its ability to mitigate its effects. The following section outlines the climatic, water resource use, agricultural, environmental and socio-economic characteristics of the Syrian Arab Republic that increase its vulnerability to drought.

A. CLIMATIC VULNERABILITY

The Syrian Arab Republic's agro-ecological zones fall into widely varying climatic, rainfall and temperature regimes, owing to differences in altitude and coastal influences. The country displays a high degree of precipitation fluctuation, as well as a high degree of aridity, and this combination increases physical vulnerability to drought. The country can be divided into five distinct agro-climatic zones, as follows (see figure V):

(a) Zone I: Covering some 2.7 million ha, or 14.6 per cent of the country, with average annual rainfall ranging from 300 to 600 mm. The common crop rotation is 50 per cent for wheat, 30-40 per cent for pulses and legumes, and 10-20 per cent for summer crops, mainly watermelon. Fallow soil is very rare;

(b) Zone II: A total area of around 2.5 million ha, or 13.3 per cent of the country's area, with annual rainfall ranging from 250-350 mm. It is possible to get two barley seasons, and deep soils are planted with wheat, pulses and summer crops;

(c) Zone III: A total area of 1.3 million ha, or 7.1 per cent of the country, with average annual rainfall of 250 mm. Barley is the main crop;

(d) Zone IV: A total area of around 1.8 million ha, or 9.9 per cent of the country, with annual rainfall of 200-250 mm. Barley is grown, but grazed in years when the yield is too low to harvest;

(e) Zone V (the Badia): A total area of 8.3 million ha, or 55.1 per cent of the country, with less than 200 mm of annual rainfall, constituting a natural grazing ground for sheep and camels.[150]

In 1998-1999, the level of rainfall received in the Syrian Arab Republic was the lowest in four decades (see chart 2). The areas worst affected were in the east, north-east, and south. Coastal areas (zone I) received more rainfall, which even exceeded the annual norm. However, rainfall in zone I was not uniform, with large differences in distribution areas, resulting in lower than average rainfall in some areas. Rainfall decline ranged from 25 per cent in some areas of zone I to 50 and 67 per cent respectively in zones IV and V.[151]

---

[150] FAO, "Special Report: FAO/WFP Crop and Food Supply Assessment Mission to the Syrian Arab Republic" (Rome, 1999), p. 5.

[151] Ibid., p. 5.

Figure V. Agro-ecological zones of the Syrian Arab Republic

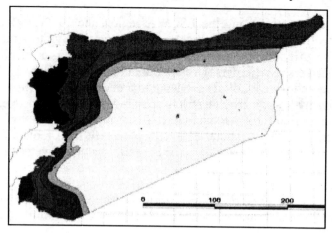

1a. Rainfall over 600 mm
1b. Rainfall 300-600 mm
2. Rainfall 250-350 mm
3. Rainfall 250 mm
4. Rainfall 200-250 mm
5. Rainfall less than 200 mm

Source: FAO, "Country Pasture/Forage Resource Profiles: Syria" (Rome, 2001).

Chart 2. 1998/99 rainfall in the Syrian Arab Republic's five agro-ecological zones against the 1989-1998 average

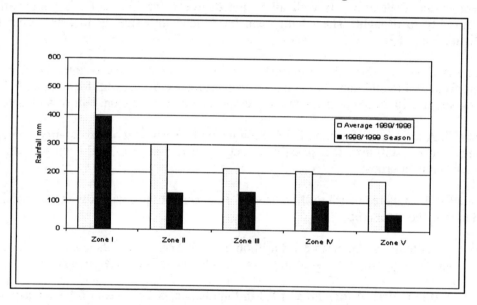

Source: FAO, "FAO/WFP Crop and Food Supply Assessment Mission to the Syrian Arab Republic" (Rome, 23 August 1999).

B. WATER RESOURCE VULNERABILITY

The Syrian Arab Republic's total renewable water resources are estimated at 21,475 million m^3. It is estimated that rainfall contributes almost 70 per cent of the available water in the country,[152] replenishing groundwater aquifers, rivers and springs that are the main sources of irrigation water. Per capita annual water use in 1997 was 1,438 m^3. Although still above the water poverty line of 1,000 m^3/person per annum, population growth and limited water resources are expected to reduce that figure to 770 m^3/person by 2025.[153] Poor management of scarce water resources amplifies the Syrian Arab Republic's vulnerability to

---

[152] Ibid.

[153] G. Somme and others, *Rainfed Wheat Productivity with Supplemental Irrigation in Al-Hasakeh, Northern Syria* (Aleppo, ICARDA and the General Commission for Scientific Agricultural Research Syria, 2005), p. 4.

drought. Over-exploitation of water resources in the northern part of the Syrian Arab Republic has reduced water supply to the south, and outdated irrigation techniques and skewed water pricing have allowed for significant water losses and mismanagement. Water use efficiency in irrigation does not exceed 50 per cent in the Syrian Arab Republic.[154] Farmers supplement surface water irrigation with groundwater withdrawals. During drought years, an increasingly noticeable drop in water tables of groundwater aquifers is recorded, as well as increasing salinity, revealing a water deficit of up to 91 per cent in north-western aquifers.[155] According to specialists at ICARDA, many Syrian farmers note that water levels drop one to three metres annually in farm groundwater wells.[156] Moreover, scarce water resources are reaching high levels of contamination: Lake Assad holds high levels of contaminants such as pesticides, fertilizer residue and salt.[157] Unaccounted for water for urban use in Damascus approaches or exceeds 50 per cent.[158] The Syrian Arab Republic had a water use sustainability indicator of 46 per cent in 1997, demonstrating water mismanagement, serious water scarcity, and the immediate need for intensive water management strategies.

The Syrian Arab Republic's surface water comes primarily from the Tigris and Euphrates River System, whose rainfall catchment area lies primarily in Turkey, providing the Tigris with 51 per cent and the Euphrates with 89 per cent respectively of the annual flow of these two rivers.[159] As a downstream riparian country with regard to these rivers, the Syrian Arab Republic is vulnerable to upstream water use, diversion projects and droughts. For example, the 1999-2000 drought sparked conflict between the Syrian Arab Republic and Turkey over decreased water flows on the Euphrates, which accounts for over 85 per cent of the Syrian Arab Republic's surface water resources, reducing flows to 160 m³/second in 2000, down from the informally agreed-upon 500 m³/second.[160] The reduced water flows caused hydropower, irrigation and agricultural losses. Turkey's Southern Anatolia Development Project (GAP) to develop a series of dams and irrigation diversions will further reduce water flows to the Syrian Arab Republic and Iraq. Conflict over the GAP programme and the associated reduced water flows has flared on several occasions, particularly during drought years. The Syrian Arab Republic's position as a downstream riparian country, dependent on 70 per cent of its surface waters from other countries, amplifies its vulnerability to drought.

C. AGRICULTURAL VULNERABILITY

Drought has had serious impacts on the agricultural sector, which utilizes 95 per cent of the Syrian Arab Republic's total water withdrawals annually.[161] The 1984 drought reduced barley yields from 1.6 million tons in 1980 to 303,500 tons in 1984.[162] In the 1980s, the Syrian Arab Republic, once a net exporter of wheat, became a net importer and the food import bill rose dramatically in 1984. The 1998/99 agricultural season was heavily affected by drought; crop yields declined drastically and significant segments of Syrian Badia herders received food aid.

---

[154] Ibid., *Micro-catchment Water Harvesting for Improved Vegetative Cover in the Syrian* Badia (Aleppo, ICARDA and the General Commission for Scientific Agricultural Research, Syria, 2005), p. 7.

[155] Abelardo Rodriguez, Hisham Salahieh, Raed Badwan and Hala Khawam, *Groundwater Use and Supplemental Irrigation in Atareb, Northwest Syria* (Aleppo, ICARDA, 1999), p. 2.

[156] Interview with Akhtar Ali Rana, Water Resources Engineer. Natural Resource Management Program at ICARDA, Aleppo, Syrian Arab Republic, 7 February 2005.

[157] E. DePauw, "Drought in WANA: six frequently asked questions", p. 2.

[158] ESCWA, *Enhancing Negotiation Skills on International Water Issues in the ESCWA Region*, p. 3.

[159] Ibid., p. 9.

[160] C. Morris, "Drought leads to water row with Turkey", *The Guardian Weekly*, 10 May 2000, p. 5.

[161] FAO, AQUASTAT Online Database (Rome, 2004), p. 3.

[162] Carter and others, "Agriculture" in Syria: A Country Study, Country Study Series, U.S. Government Printing Office, 1988.

In the Syrian Arab Republic, there are an estimated 6 million ha of cultivable land, of which 5.5 million ha are farmed.[163] Of the cultivable lands in use, approximately 76 per cent are rain-fed, while 24 per cent are irrigated.[164] Of the irrigated lands, many are also still dependent on rainfall, the amount of which is highly variable by region and by season, making rain-fed farming extremely risky and influencing cropping systems and production. Areas with comparatively high precipitation are cropped with wheat and legumes, while only barley is cultivated in low rainfall areas. Expansion of irrigation systems could decrease the risks associated with rain-fed farming, as well as increase yields. However, irrigation offers limited protection from the impacts of drought. The 1999 drought reduced the Syrian barley harvest to 380,000 tons, less than half of 1998's total and down 72 per cent from the previous five-year average.[165] The drought's impact on wheat production, although significant, was less severe, as 40 per cent of Syrian wheat fields are irrigated.[166] Nevertheless, the wheat harvest in 1999 was one third less than the previous year's crop and 28 per cent below average.[167] Although extension and improvement of irrigation systems could substantially reduce drought risk and raise agricultural output, the problems associated with irrigation, including irrigation water losses, outdated irrigation systems, increased soil salinity, water logging, over-exploitation of water resources and overall land degradation, remain a challenge in the Syrian Arab Republic.

The 8.3 million ha of rangeland in the Badia were equally hard hit; this is where most of the Syrian Arab Republic's nomadic herders and sheep flocks are located. In non-drought years, the Badia's livestock-based production systems provide about two thirds of the red meat and a third of the milk production of the country.[168] Natural vegetation of the Badia, which is rainfall-dependent, constitutes a significant portion of feed for the livestock, which was devastated by the 1999 drought, reducing vegetation per ha from 165 kg/ha to virtually zero.[169] The combined impact of drought-induced Badia vegetation desiccation and the decline in grain production and crop residues resulted in a lack of feed for livestock and widespread under-nutrition and disease in the sheep population. Many herders lost their livestock to disease and starvation, as the barley crop collapse severely limited the feed available. The 1998-1999 mortality rates for mature ewes and lambs were 10 per cent and 25 per cent respectively, higher than the average of 3-4 per cent.[170] It is estimated that, in 1999, herders sold over 65 per cent of their herds and accumulated debts equivalent to three times their income in normal years.[171] Although the Syrian Government imported barley to alleviate the feed shortage caused by the collapse of the barley crop in 1999, the economic slowdown, largely the result of falling oil prices, meant that it could only import 200,000 tons, leaving a shortfall of nearly 1 million tons.[172]

D. ENVIRONMENTAL VULNERABILITY

The Syrian Badia is most environmentally vulnerable to drought. Rainfall is the primary source of freshwater, as groundwater in this area is very limited. From 1997 to 2001, the Badia received about 67 per cent less rainfall than the average,[173] resulting in the virtual decimation of herbage from Badia vegetation, reducing capacity for regeneration of forage plants, and the ability of the soils to resist wind erosion and desertification. Consecutive droughts have considerably reduced the declining biomass and vegetation cover and the Badia's carrying capacity.

---

[163] FAO, "FAO/WFP Crop and Food Supply Assessment Mission to the Syrian Arab Republic", p. 4.

[164] Ibid., p. 5.

[165] Ibid., p. 2.

[166] Ibid., p. 5.

[167] FAO, "Drought conditions threaten food security of Syria's nomadic livestock producers".

[168] G. Somme and others, "Micro-Catchment Water Harvesting for Improved Vegetative Cover in the Syrian Badia" (Aleppo, ICARDA, 1999), p. 28.

[169] Ibid., p. 6.

[170] FAO, "Drought conditions threaten food security of Syria's nomadic livestock producers".

[171] FAO, "FAO/WFP Crop and Food Supply Assessment Mission to the Syrian Arab Republic", p. 13.

[172] Ibid., p. 3.

[173] G. Somme and others, "Micro-catchment Water Harvesting for Improved Vegetative Cover in the Syrian Badia", p. 6.

Human-induced land degradation and increased desertification have resulted in wildlife habitat and biodiversity losses. Poor land use patterns coupled with drought have resulted in increased land degradation and desertification, increasing environmental vulnerability to drought. The problem is most acute in the Badia. The traditional Syrian pastoral migration system of moving to less arid areas during the summer, and back to the Badia at the onset of the rains, allowed for the regeneration of forage plants in the Badia. However, the introduction of farming marginal land and using transported water and feed to keep flocks on the pasture at unseasonable times have led to constant pressure on the Badia lands, reducing the amount of organic matter build-up, and increasing the rate of deterioration of grazing lands. The result is that herders are able to keep sheep roaming the Badia all year round, causing eradication of new growth of potential shrubs. The Badia, once able to provide the majority of feed for sheep, now only provides 20 to 25 per cent.[174]

Until the 1940s, flocks of gazelle (*Gazella subgutturosa marica*) and oryx (*Oryx leucoryx*) were seen in the Badia, and vegetation was composed of climax plants such as *Salsola vermiculata, Atriplex leucoclada, Artemisia herba-alba,* and *Stipa barbata.*[175] However, widespread deterioration of rangelands and loss of wildlife habitats have placed these indigenous species under serious threat. Despite efforts by the Government to mitigate the degradation of the Badia, such as the provision of forage banks, surface dams and planting shrubs over millions of ha, the vegetation of the Badia continues to deteriorate. Low vegetation leads to soil, water, and wind erosion, resulting in further decline of the micro-climate and thereby increasing vulnerability to drought.

E. SOCIO-ECONOMIC VULNERABILITY

The Syrian economy can be characterized as more diversified than other economies of the region. Syrian industry includes textiles, food-processing, beverages, tobacco, phosphate rock mining, and petroleum. However, the Syrian Arab Republic is a largely State-run economy, heavily dependent on oil and gas for foreign exchange earnings (60-70 per cent of export earnings), and agriculture for employment and food security. As such, the Syrian economy is highly vulnerable to external shocks such as drops in world oil prices and drought. It is estimated that the collapse in world oil prices in 1998 reduced the value of Syrian oil exports by around 35 per cent, while overall oil-related earnings in 1998 were 30 per cent lower than in 1997.[176] The 1999 drought reduced agricultural production significantly, affecting GDP. The combination of drought and the fall in world oil prices also adversely impacted the Government's ability to finance free or subsidized services, such as education and health, and subsidized medicines and basic food items, including bread and sugar.

The high population growth in the Syrian Arab Republic is placing increasing pressure on the country's natural and economic resources. Population growth has generated increased demand for livestock and agricultural products, resulting in unprecedented pressure on arable and pasture lands. Although population growth is projected to slow to 2.2 per cent for the period 2002-2015, fertility rates remain high, and a significant portion of the population is under the age of 15. Currently, the country's rapidly growing population adds an estimated 140,000 to the numbers of those seeking employment, further increasing the high unemployment rates.[177] The lack of economic opportunities has encouraged considerable emigration, as a number of Syrian nationals work abroad. Economic growth has not been able to make a dent in the unemployment rate, nor adequately absorb the drought-induced rural-urban migration, while off-farm employment, a traditional drought-coping mechanism for agricultural labour, is difficult to find.

Until the mid-1970s, agriculture had been the Syrian Arab Republic's primary economic activity and was the most important sector of the economy and the fastest growing sector in the 1940s and 1950s.

---

[174] Ibid., p. 7.

[175] FAO and the World Bank, *Farming Systems and Poverty: Improving Farmers' Livelihoods in a Changing World*, box 3.13, "Range rehabilitation in pastoral farming systems".

[176] FAO, "FAO/WFP Crop and Food Supply Assessment Mission to the Syrian Arab Republic", p. 4.

[177] Ibid., p. 4.

Although slowly conceding its economic position to oil, gas, and manufacturing, agriculture remains a major employer and contributor to GDP. Currently the agricultural value added represents almost a quarter of GDP (23.5 per cent in 2002), which is the highest in the ESCWA region. This makes the agricultural sector, and economy as a whole, vulnerable to drought. In 1999 and 2000, Syrian GDP growth was -1.8 per cent and 0.60 per cent respectively, in part because of the adverse effects of drought on agricultural production.[178]

Half the population of the Syrian Arab Republic live in rural areas and are largely dependent on agriculture for their livelihood. The agricultural sector employs 32 per cent of the Syrian labour force. Of the rural populations, the Badia herders are most vulnerable to, and have been most severely affected by, drought. Economic development in the Badia has been slow, and access to Government services is limited. The Badia's nomadic population of 900,000 consists mainly of herders and semi-settled farmers.[179] The estimated income per capita is 60 per cent below the national average, and family size is larger than average, with about 7 to 12 members.[180] About half of the nomads in the Badia rely exclusively on sheep rearing for their livelihood. For herders, meat and dairy products are the main source of income, while semi-settled farmers grow barley as well. In non-drought years, Badia households produce an annual income of around 150,000 to 200,000 Syrian pounds (US$ 3,300 to US$ 4,300), allowing them to meet food and investment needs.[181] The high animal mortality rates and higher feed prices sharply reduced income from sheep and sheep products, thus drastically reducing the household incomes of Badia herders. Distress sales of animals at depressed prices and increased livestock disease, starvation and mortality resulted in significant flock losses and household wealth loss. Many herders lost entire flocks and migrated to urban areas in search of employment. However, opportunities were limited in an economy hard hit by recession. Small herders were most seriously impacted by the drought. In June 1999, FAO estimated small herders had sold over 65 per cent of their sheep and accumulated debts equivalent to three times their annual income.[182]

Badia women have been equally vulnerable to the drought, since their ability to mobilize resources to feed their families is extremely limited. The instability of nomadic life, the lack of Government services such as health care, and the general remoteness all exacerbate the vulnerability of women and children in the Badia. As household income declined during the 1999 drought, many families began reducing their caloric intake. Malnourishment, according to FAO, was most pronounced among poorer Badia women and children. Herders and their families were generally unprepared for the worst drought in four decades, and exhausted all coping strategies. In 1999, FAO estimated that about a third of the Badia population were in need of emergency food assistance owing to the adverse impacts of the drought.

The urban population, although not as severely affected by the drought, nevertheless felt its impact. Increased rural-urban migration placed increasing pressure on urban areas and services, with increasing levels of urban poverty and unemployment as consequences. Lower crop yields due to drought translated into higher food prices in urban markets, leading to higher per capita food expenditure, at a time of economic recession. Water shortages were experienced in urban areas, where rationing became common practice. In Damascus, water was cut off to the city's 2 million residents several nights a week during the 1999-2001 drought. The water shortages exacerbated the adverse impacts on public health and resulted in reduced sewage flows, increased pollutant concentrations, and increased incidence of water-borne diseases.

F. DROUGHT EARLY WARNING AND MITIGATION IN THE SYRIAN ARAB REPUBLIC

The 1999 drought, the most severe the Syrian Arab Republic had encountered in 40 years, left few untouched. FAO and the World Food Programme (WFP) instituted an emergency relief programme geared primarily to Badia herders. In view of the severity of the drought, the Government implemented a number of emergency measures, including:
  (a) Importing and distributing free medicine and vaccination for sheep;
  (b) Providing extra feed rations to sheep herders, on a subsidized and deferred payment basis;

---

[178] ESCWA, *Survey of Economic and Social Developments in the ESCWA Region, 2001-2002* (E/ESCWA/ED/2002/8), p. 5.

[179] FAO, "FAO/WFP Crop and Food Supply Assessment Mission to the Syrian Arab Republic", p. 12.

[180] Ibid., p. 12.

[181] Ibid.

[182] Ibid., p. 13.

(c) Providing extra financial resources to the revolving fund for feed, as well as price supports;

(d) Providing water for humans and animals in the Badia region;

(e) Authorizing the Fodder Establishment to import additional barley;

(f) Allowing grazing in conservation reserves, which are normally protected;

(g) Allowing private sector imports of feed, particularly barley.[183]

Government response to drought has been reactionary, as no early warning system or national drought preparedness plan exists. The seriousness of the drought emphasizes the necessity of developing strategies to mitigate future drought occurrences, which the Syrian Government has expressed interest in developing. The key challenges to establishing a drought preparedness plan in the Syrian Arab Republic are outlined below.

1. *Institutional capacity*

Currently, three ministries are involved in water supply, management, and use: the Ministry of Agriculture and Agrarian Reform, the Ministry of Irrigation, and the Ministry of the Environment. Within these ministries, General Commissions on Agriculture, Scientific Research, and Hydrological Design also work on water and drought issues. However, institutional arrangements for drought monitoring and drought early warning are lacking in the Syrian Arab Republic. Moreover, the country does not have socio-economic drought-monitoring focal points or institutions that could act as a central coordination unit for data, analysis and information dissemination. Drought vulnerability assessments are not conducted, nor are any early warning bulletins issued to vulnerable communities.[184] Drought monitoring is not conducted, but rather attention is focused on monitoring the supply of water within the country. Response to drought is not institutionalized, and responses have been ad hoc and crisis-oriented.[185] Water demand management has largely not been instituted in the Syrian Arab Republic, as water supply is largely regarded as a right by the public, and water pricing is politically charged. Irrigation water is provided at no cost to farmers, while urban water is supplied at US$ 0.10/m^3, regardless of water availability. Integrated water resources management remains a challenge for the Syrian Government, since significant changes in the institutional structures would be necessary to enable a more multidisciplinary and integrated approach to drought monitoring and early warning.

2. *Technical capacity and monitoring*

In any drought monitoring system, meteorological services play a key role. Data are sparse, and most climatic stations are located in predominantly agricultural areas, and usually not located in more arid and less populated areas such as the Badia. This poses a problem, as the Badia is the agro-ecological zone most vulnerable to drought in the Syrian Arab Republic. In general, there is also a lack of analytical tools for drought monitoring, a lack of harmonized suitable information products, and a lack of information-sharing in the Syrian Arab Republic. Hydrological and meteorological data networks do not share information, which is generally considered classified, is outdated by up to one year, and is in many cases unreliable.[186] However, the Ministry of Irrigation in the Syrian Arab Republic recently instituted, in collaboration with the Japan International Cooperation Agency (JICA), a watershed GIS monitoring system.[187] Although remote sensing technology and GIS have significant potential to address the data and knowledge gaps, the technical capacity to interpret this data for subsequent introduction in decision-making is still lacking.

---

[183] FAO, "FAO/WFP Crop and Food Supply Assessment Mission to the Syrian Arab Republic".

[184] E. DePauw, "Drought Early Warning Systems in West Asia and North Africa".

[185] Interview with Jamal Jamaleddin, Director of Training, Research, and International Projects, Ministry of Irrigation, Damascus, Syrian Arab Republic, 28 February 2005.

[186] Interview with Akhtar Ali Rana, Water Resources Engineer, Natural Resource Management Program, ICARDA, Aleppo, Syrian Arab Republic, 27 February 2005.

[187] Interview with Jamal Jamaleddin, Director of Training, Research, and International Projects, Ministry of Irrigation, Damascus, Syrian Arab Republic, 28 February 2005.

VII. YEMEN

The 1990-1991 drought had a heavy impact on the Yemeni economy and population. The agricultural sector registered significant yield losses, resulting in widespread farm losses and increased poverty in rural areas, and reducing agricultural income contribution to GDP. The drought highlighted the vital role that adequate rainfall and water resources play in keeping Yemen's economy profitable and sustainable, as Yemen has no perennial rivers and depends on rainfall from wadi run-off and groundwater recharge. The drought had serious repercussions on the food security of a large segment of the population. According to the World Bank, a sizeable portion of the population remains economically vulnerable to falling into poverty due to drought, as the Yemeni agricultural sector provides employment for 58 per cent of the population and a livelihood for 77 per cent.[188] Compounding the problem, the 1990-1991 drought coincided with the 1991 Gulf war, which prompted the return of 800,000 Yemeni workers from the Gulf States, leading to a significant loss of workers' remittances. These shocks in the early 1990s resulted in lower economic growth, greater financial imbalances, lower worker remittances, and higher inflation and external debt. These negative impacts reduced Yemen's resilience to drought and the country's ability to mitigate its effects. The following section outlines the climatic, water resource use, agricultural, environmental, social and economic characteristics of Yemen that increase its vulnerability to drought.

A. CLIMATIC VULNERABILITY

Yemen can be divided into three main agro-ecological zones (see figure VI).[189]

Figure VI. Agro-ecological zones of Yemen

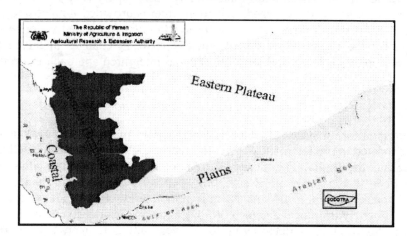

Source: FAO, "Yemen national report" (Rome, Food and Agriculture Organization of the United Nations, 6 June 2002), available at: http://www.fao.org/ag/agl/swlwpnr/reports/y_nr/z_ye/ye.htm.

(a) *Coastal zone*: This zone is characterized by wadis and flood plains with agricultural land, much of which is cultivated. Rainfall ranges from 50-300 mm annually.[190] Cultivated fields provide a major source of forage for livestock, while fallow land and harvested fields are valuable grazing areas. The coastal zone suffers from shallow aquifer depletion and seawater intrusion due to increased groundwater abstraction, deteriorating spate irrigation[191] and water harvesting structures;

(b) *Mountainous highlands*: The Highlands are Yemen's main rain-fed agricultural areas, growing mainly cereals and pulses, with some vegetable and fruit orchards. In addition, the most productive pastures

[188] World Bank. *Republic of Yemen Poverty Update* (Washington, D.C., 11 December 2002), p. iii.

[189] A.A. Alabsi, "Country Pasture/Forage Resource Profiles: Yemen" (Rome, FAO, November, 2001).

[190] FAO, "Yemen national report" (Rome, 6 June 2002), p. 9.

[191] Spate irrigation is conducted by capturing and diverting periodic floodwaters.

with terrace systems form the main part of the Highlands, making it the most important area for livestock production. The cropping pattern is based on cereals and pulses in the rainy season from June to August; the land is used for grazing in winter. Since the inter-mountain plains and basins receive limited rainfall, supplementary irrigation is needed for most of the year, leading to increased construction of wells and to aquifer depletion. This zone enjoys moderate to high rainfall, on average 300-500 mm/year, but reaching more than 1,000 mm/year in some areas;[192]

(c) *Eastern Desert Plateau*: This zone is semi-arid with no distinct rainy seasons and covers vast expanses of sand desert and dissected plateau, with elevation ranging from 500 m on its northern and southern sides, to about 2,400 m on its western side.[193] Annual rainfall is well below 200 mm, the minimum requirement for rain-fed crop cultivation.[194] Water supply depends on limited, erratic rainfall over vast desert grazing land where camels and goats feed in the eastern plain for three to four months a year.

Yemen has a semi-arid to arid climate, with rainy seasons in spring and summer. Yemen's agro-ecological zones fall into widely varying climatic, rainfall and temperature regimes, due to differences in altitude and coastal influences. The country displays a high degree of precipitation fluctuation, as well as aridity, particularly inland, the combination of which increases vulnerability to drought. Rainfall rises from less than 50 mm along the Red Sea and Gulf of Aden coasts to a maximum of 500-800 mm in the Western Highlands and decreases steadily to below 50 mm inland.[195] Drought has its hardest impact in February and March.[196]

B. WATER RESOURCE VULNERABILITY

Water in Yemen is available from wadis, springs, shallow wells, boreholes and traditional cisterns that collect run-off. Groundwater constitutes the majority of total renewable water resources, while rainfall is the major source of all water in the country. Renewable water resources were an estimated 4,900 m^3 or 206 m^3 per person in 2002, well below the critical water scarcity level of 500 m^3 per person per year. The distribution of water is erratic, with 90 per cent of the population having less than a minimum standard of domestic supply.[197] Yemen's per capita water availability compares with other countries of the Arabian Peninsula and Jordan. However, unlike the Gulf countries, Yemen has limited water desalination capacity to compensate for water shortages. The quantity of desalinated water was estimated at 10 million m^3/year in 1989, contributing to the water supply of Aden.[198] As a result of very high population growth, expansion of irrigated areas, and rapid industrial growth, pressure on Yemen's scarce water resources is acute. Water withdrawal in Yemen exceeds sustainable levels by 30 per cent.[199] With population continuing to grow at high rates, Yemen's water resources are being pumped and are diminishing at alarming rates. Owing to Yemen's scarce and limited water resources and high dependence on rainfall, it is particularly vulnerable to drought.

Yemen's vulnerability to drought is magnified by the poor management of scarce and overexploited water resources. The agriculture sector is by far the major consumer of water and, since it is not priced, water use efficiency in the agricultural sector is very low. Outdated and poorly maintained irrigation systems have allowed for significant water losses and mismanagement: water use efficiency in irrigation does not exceed

---

[192] FAO, "Yemen national report", p. 7.

[193] Ibid., p. 10.

[194] A.A. Alabsi, "Country Pasture/Forage Resource Profiles: Yemen" (Rome, FAO, November 2001), p. 8.

[195] Ibid., p. 6.

[196] Interview with Isma'il Muharram, Chairman of Agricultural Research and Extension Authority, Sana'a, Yemen, 7 March 2005.

[197] World Bank, "Country Brief: Middle East & North Africa Region (MENA) - Yemen" (Washington, D.C., 2005).

[198] FAO, "Yemen national report", p. 15.

[199] Ibid., p. 13.

30 per cent in Yemen. Farmers supplement spate irrigation with groundwater withdrawals using tube-well technology, leading to the rapid development of groundwater irrigation and increased aquifer depletion. The problem of unsustainable groundwater extraction has been caused by the rapid spread of groundwater irrigation, combined with dwindling rates of recharge, in part due to recurrent droughts. The rate of decline of the groundwater levels is alarmingly high in many zones, especially in the Yemen Highlands, where declines of between 2 and 6 m/year are commonly observed.[200] In the Sa'adah and Amran basins, aquifer depletion is at the rate of 2-8 metres per year. Since 1992 the number of boreholes in Sana'a Governorate alone has increased from 600 to 5,000[201] since no government restrictions or controls are imposed. In coastal zones, over-exploitation has led to the increased incidence of saltwater intrusion.[202] Moreover, competition among water users for available limited supplies is becoming intense, leading to conflicts among stakeholders.[203] For example, in 1999, 700 soldiers were dispatched to quell the clashes that claimed six lives and injured 60 in fights between two villages disputing rights to a spring near Ta'iz.[204] The two villages fought over conflicting claims to the spring water: one claimed exclusive rights as it was located on its property, while the other claimed rights based on a 50-year-old court verdict. Yemen's water scarcity only stresses the need for improved water resource management with increased stakeholder participation.

C. AGRICULTURAL VULNERABILITY

The agricultural sector withdraws 95 per cent of Yemen's total water resource withdrawal annually, followed by domestic and industrial use. Of Yemen's total land area, only 3.2 per cent is arable or permanent cropland.[205] Of the cultivated land, only 29.5 per cent is irrigated by spate, tube-well, and spring-well irrigation. Irrigated farming systems are still heavily dependent on rainfall, especially those under spate irrigation systems. Agricultural production and productivity in Yemen rain-fed areas are extremely low, in large part because of rainfall variations. For example, cereal yields are fairly low, between 0.6 and 1.6 tons/ha, averaging 1.2 tons/ha, or about 50 per cent lower than in other countries in the region.[206] This is in part due to the fact that farmers plant more drought-resistant crops that have lower yields, to mitigate the risks of low rainfall and water shortages.[207] Drought exacerbates these production variations in rain-fed production systems, including barley, millet and sorghum. Cereal yields have declined 66 per cent since 1979-1981,[208] but they remain the major crop, covering about 600,000 ha in 2000, or 54 per cent of cultivated area.[209] The 1990-1991 drought reduced barley, millet and sorghum yields by 38 per cent, 33 per cent and 34 per cent respectively in 1991 compared with 1989.[210] Crop yields recovered in subsequent years, registering good growth in 1997-1998 thanks to good rainfall. Expansion of irrigation systems could decrease the risks associated with rain-fed farming, as well as increase yields. During the 1990-1991 drought, vegetables largely cultivated under irrigated farming systems, registered a smaller drop in production (16 per cent in 1991 compared with 1989). However, Yemen does not have adequate water resources to expand irrigation at current water use rates. Problems associated with irrigation, such as water

---

[200] Ibid., p. 15.

[201] Interview with Ibrahim Thabet, Director, FAO-Yemen, Sana'a, 7 March 2005.

[202] FAO, "Yemen national report".

[203] UNDP, Sustainable Water Resources Management: Programme Outline, UNDP - Yemen, 9 July 1997.

[204] M.H. Al-Qadhi, "Thirst for water and development leads to conflict in Yemen", *Choices, The Human Development Magazine*, March 2003 (New York, UNDP).

[205] World Resources Institute (WRI), "Agriculture and Food - Yemen", EarthTrends Country Profiles, EarthTrends Online Database, Washington, D.C., 2004, p. 1.

[206] A.A. Alabsi, "Country Pasture/Forage Resource Profiles: Yemen" (Rome, FAO, November 2001), p. 3.

[207] Interview with Naji Abu Hatim, Senior Rural Development Specialist, Department of Rural Development, Water & Environment, World Bank, Sana'a, Yemen, 7 March 2005.

[208] World Resources Institute, "Agriculture and Food - Yemen", p. 1.

[209] A.A. Alabsi, "Country Pasture/Forage Resource Profiles: Yemen" (Rome, FAO, November 2001), p. 3.

[210] FAOSTAT Online Database (Rome, FAO, 2004).

losses, outdated and derelict systems, increased soil salinity, water logging, and over-exploitation of water resources remain significant challenges to water security and drought resilience in Yemen.

The rangeland occupying most (75 per cent) of Yemen's land area was also seriously affected by the drought.[211] Yemen's pastures contribute to 53 per cent of the total sheep and goat feed requirements, with the deficit covered by grazing cropland and stubble, fallow land and supplementary feeds.[212] Combined with reduced fodder production due to drought, herders depending on the vegetation of these pastures had insufficient feed for their livestock, thereby losing their livestock to disease and starvation, while others were forced to liquidate their livestock assets, by selling them for premature slaughter. The slaughter of sheep and goats in Yemen in 1992, compared with 1989, increased by 11 per cent, and returned to pre-drought levels by 1994.[213] This greatly affected agricultural production, as livestock contribute 20 per cent to agricultural GDP.[214]

Insufficient rainfall remains the major obstacle to increased agricultural productivity, and hence increased food security.[215] Owing to population growth and limited agricultural growth, Yemen continues to increase its food import bill yearly. Since much of Yemen's agricultural production is rain-fed, drought can be highly detrimental to the agricultural sector and Yemen's food security. Given its high level of food aid dependence, which peaked at 6.1 per cent in 2002, Yemen is particularly vulnerable to drought-induced agricultural crises.

D. ENVIRONMENTAL VULNERABILITY

The biodiversity of Yemen is threatened by deforestation, major drops in water tables, and massive erosion of the highland terrace ecosystems. The accelerating degradation of watershed basins has serious economic, ecological, environmental and social implications, which reduce Yemen's resilience to drought. Most watershed areas show extensive soil erosion and desertification, due to poor land use and recurrent droughts. Where water resources have dried up, the agricultural lands that have been consequently abandoned account for about 25 per cent of the country's arable land.[216] Terracing walls have fallen into disrepair and collapse, permitting soil erosion, and limiting the ability of the terraces to harness moisture for crops or fruit trees, thereby increasing vulnerability to desertification and drought. Almost half of Yemen's land area is suffering from severe human-induced land degradation.[217] Desertification, exacerbated by drought, is one of the country's most serious problems, since it is estimated that 92.8 per cent of the country is at risk of desertification[218] owing to decreases in plant cover and changes in the micro-climate that result in reduced rainfall, higher temperatures, and hot winds, carrying sand from the desert and permanently changing the climate of areas vulnerable to degradation and desertification such as the terraced highlands, the intensively cropped coastal areas, and the over-grazed Eastern Plateau.[219] These micro-climate changes have increased the incidence of drought and reduced area-specific water renewal rates.[220]

---

[211] A.A. Alabsi, "Country Pasture/Forage Resource Profiles: Yemen"(Rome, FAO, November 2001), p. 3.

[212] Ibid.

[213] FAOSTAT Online Database 2004.

[214] A.A. Alabsi, "Country Pasture/Forage Resource Profiles: Yemen" (Rome, FAO, November 2001), p. 4.

[215] ESCWA, *Review and Appraisal of Progress Made by Yemen in the Implementation of the New Programme of Action for the Least Developed Countries for the 1990s* (E/ESCWA/ED/2001/17).

[216] A. Aw-Hassan, M. Alsanabani and A.R. Bamatraf, "Step forward, Yemen terraces", ICARDA *Caravan* 10, (Aleppo, 1999), p. 1.

[217] FAO, Terrastat Online Database, Rome, 2004.

[218] Abdulmalik Althawr, "Contribution to the Agriculture Sector Review in Yemen". Ministry of Agriculture and Irrigation, Yemen, February 1999, p. 21.

[219] Interview with Naji Abu Hatim, Senior Rural Development Specialist, Department of Rural Development, Water & Environment, World Bank, Sana'a, Yemen, 7 March 2005.

[220] Ibid.

Low rainfall and recurrent droughts contribute to and accelerate overgrazing in the rangelands, particularly in the coastal rangelands and Eastern Plateau where livestock graze intensively,[221] thereby increasing pressure on productivity. Drought accelerates desertification and the total clearance of biomass, as livestock graze the limited rangeland vegetation available during drought, which in turn increases soil fragility, and wind and water erosion. Excessive erosion has reduced soil cover, water holding capacity and water retention, thereby increasing vulnerability to desertification in Yemen.

E. SOCIO-ECONOMIC VULNERABILITY

The Yemeni economy can be characterized as agriculturally based and oil exporting. Despite the availability of oil, Yemen remains one of the least developed countries in the world and ranks 148 out of 175 countries on the UNDP Human Development Index (2003).[222] Economic growth is fuelled by the oil and agricultural sectors. During the post-reform period of 1996-2001, economic growth was driven mostly by agriculture, which grew at the rate of 5 per cent per year.[223] Agriculture contributed 15 per cent of GDP in 2003; however, this contribution underestimates the importance of agriculture in the economy, since an important share of secondary and tertiary activities are agriculture-related. Agriculture also contributes to a third of the non-oil merchandize exports,[224] while oil accounts for 87 per cent of goods and services exported and 70 per cent of Government revenues.[225] Yemen's dependence on oil and agriculture for economic growth increase its vulnerability to external shocks such as oil price changes and drought. Given the high rate of socio-economic dependence on the agricultural sector, the most water-dependent sector of the economy, Yemen's economy shows very low resilience to socio-economic drought and drought crises.

Furthermore, Yemen's population growth rate is the highest in the ESCWA region, and one of the highest in the world, projected at 3.6 per cent for the period 2002-2015.[226] Yemen's growing population is exerting pressure on its already scarce water resources for both increasing domestic water requirements and agricultural sector demand for increased food production. The population pyramid of Yemen shows 49 per cent of the population under the age of 15, translating into unabated pressure on the scarce water and land resources of the region. Population growth has surpassed the water resources' sustainable carrying capacity by 30 per cent, as demonstrated by diminishing water quality in groundwater aquifers, the loss of valuable water resources, and ever-decreasing water per capita availability rates. At another level, Yemen has one of the highest fertility rates in the world of 7 births per family. As a result, Yemeni households have a large number of children, which increases households' economic vulnerability to poverty in case of a shock such as drought. Poverty and malnutrition of children is associated with environmental endowments; 42 per cent of Yemen's population lives in poverty, and another 25 per cent is economically vulnerable and lies just above the poverty line.[227] Limited access to basic services and high unemployment, estimated at 40 per cent, further contribute to poverty.[228] With the working-age population growing 3.8 per cent each year, current levels of investment and employment growth do not generate enough jobs to absorb new entrants.[229] Yemen's dependence on oil revenue has limited employment creation opportunities and investment in non-oil industries. Employment is largely limited to agricultural activities, with limited non-agricultural employment economy-wide. However, monthly wages in agriculture are 41 per cent lower than in manufacturing, 58 per cent lower than in construction, and 67 per cent less than in the hotel and restaurant

---

[221] A.A. Alabsi, "Country Pasture/Forage Resource Profiles: Yemen" (Rome, FAO, November, 2001).

[222] World Bank, "Country Brief: Middle East & North Africa Region (MENA) - Yemen" (Washington, D.C., 2005).

[223] World Bank, *Republic of Yemen Poverty Update* (Washington, D.C., 11 December 2002), p. 20.

[224] Ibid., "Yemen - Rainfed Agriculture and Livestock: Rural Poverty Alleviation Project", Project Information Document, World Bank, Washington, D.C., 2005.

[225] Ibid., "Country Brief: Middle East & North Africa Region (MENA) - Yemen".

[226] Ibid., *Republic of Yemen Poverty Update*, p. 28.

[227] Ibid., p. ii.

[228] Ibid., "Country Brief: Middle East & North Africa Region (MENA) - Yemen".

[229] Ibid.

sector.[230] Poverty is most pronounced in rural areas, where 83 per cent of the poor live and depend on agriculture for livelihood.[231] Poverty has increased, in part because of water shortages in the agricultural sector in the 1990s, thereby making the rural poor the most vulnerable to drought. The agricultural sector provides employment for 58 per cent and livelihoods for 77 per cent of the population.[232] However, employment figures disguise the actual economic dependence on agriculture, as many children and women engage in unpaid agricultural employment in Yemen: 88 per cent of the female labour force.[233]

Within the agricultural sector, irrigated agriculture remains the main economic activity and source of income and employment in rural areas. The depletion of groundwater, whether human- or drought-induced, directly affects poverty, employment and social order. Moreover, nearly 80 per cent of farms are either pure livestock-producing, or mixed livestock and cultivated farming, with a ratio of 59 per cent for mixed farming and 20 per cent for pure livestock farming.[234] Livestock is also a major source of cash income for households with inadequate landholdings, where women are largely responsible for duties related to livestock.[235] Livestock farmers tend to be poorer farmers, as the rural poor have easier access to livestock than to land or water rights. Pasture-fed livestock breeding has been traditionally practised and is a prominent feature of rural economy and agricultural activities in many parts of Yemen. Owing to the high stocking rates of livestock on Yemen's arable and rangelands, and because of the poverty and dependence on rain-fed pastures, livestock farmers are extremely vulnerable to drought. Drought also affects the majority (77 per cent) of the population and drought-induced labour flows out of agriculture become difficult to absorb in other sectors of the economy. This is particularly salient, as Yemen's oil sector is unable to provide comparable employment. Rural populations, landless livestock farmers, and women, and children in particular, without access to social services such as water, education and health care, are therefore most vulnerable to drought-related disasters.

Yemen's overall food self-sufficiency covers a third of the need of the national economy for food. However, Yemen's fast-growing population and limited agricultural growth places increased reliance on food imports. Cereal imports increased 48.5 per cent between 1961 and 1991, and constituted 75 per cent of domestic consumption in the period 1992-2002.[236] Yemen has also increased its dependence on food aid, which constituted 2.9 per cent of domestic consumption in 1970-1980, increased to 4.2 per cent in 1981-1991, and still further to 6.1 per cent in 2002,[237] making Yemen one of the most food-aid dependent countries in the ESCWA region. A recent food insecurity survey revealed that approximately 48 per cent of the Yemeni population is generally food insecure, with 22 per cent definitely food insecure.[238] The prevalence of food insecurity is higher in the Governorates of Shabwah, Sa'adah, Hajjar, Ibb, and Mahrah, which reflects vulnerability by agro-ecological zone. Large households in desert and coastal regions are slightly more likely to be food insecure with moderate and severe hunger compared with mountain regions, while small livestock and landless farmers tend to be more vulnerable while, within the household, females are most food insecure.[239]

---

[230] Ibid., *Republic of Yemen Poverty Update*, p. iv.

[231] Ibid., p. v.

[232] Ibid., p. iii.

[233] ESCWA, *Where do Arab Women Stand in the Development Process? A Gender-Based Statistical Analysis*, p. 14.

[234] A. A. Alabsi, "Country Pasture/Forage Resource Profiles: Yemen" (Rome, FAO, 2001), p. 7.

[235] World Bank, "Yemen - Rainfed Agriculture and Livestock: Rural Poverty Alleviation Project", Project Information Document, World Bank, Washington, D.C., 2005.

[236] J.P. Wilson and H.J. Bruins, "Food security in the Middle East since 1961" Jacob Blaustein Institute for Desert Research, Ben- Gurion University of the Negev, Sede Boqer, Israel, 2005, pp. 2 and 4.

[237] Ibid., p. 4.

[238] Interview with Ibrahim Thabet, Program Director, FAO - Yemen, Sana'a, Yemen, 7 March 2005.

[239] Ibid.

Yemen's limited water supply leaves 90 per cent of the population with less than a minimum standard of domestic supply,[240] and poor access to safe drinking water and sanitation are threats to public health.[241] It is estimated that only 44 per cent of the population have access to the main water supply and only 12 per cent to safe sanitation,[242] and women and girls still walk for hours every day to collect water.[243] The rate of groundwater mining in the country is creating a high poverty risk for rural communities and accelerating rural-urban migration. Major urban centres, such as Sana'a, ration water and distribute it only once every four days. The urban utility in Sana'a, the National Water and Sanitation Authority (NWSA), is unable to keep pace with new housing and industrial development. This growing water shortage is a principal challenge to poverty reduction and improved public health, since water shortages result in reduced sewage flows, increased pollutant concentrations, and worsening environmental health. The incidence of diarrhoea has not abated in recent years, in large part owing to low connectivity to sewerage systems, erratic water supply, and water shortage during drought.

F. DROUGHT EARLY WARNING AND MITIGATION IN YEMEN

Owing to Yemen's low socio-economic resilience to drought, the 1990-1991 drought left few unaffected, and was perhaps the worst drought in Yemen's recent history. In view of the severity of the socio-economic impacts of the 1990-1991 drought and subsequent droughts, and the linkages to poverty, food security, agricultural policy, and water resource policy, the Government of Yemen has taken steps to mitigate the water shortage situation in Yemen since 1991, including the following:

(a) Creating a single water resource management agency, the National Water Resources Authority;

(b) Institutionalizing water conservation programmes such as fog collection, water harvesting, water treatment and reuse, dams, and water rationing;

(c) Improving access to sanitation with increased connectivity to sewerage infrastructure;

(d) Institutionalizing food security programmes, such as the credit subsidy for wheat and flour, diesel fuel for water pumps, groundwater irrigation, and maintenance subsidy for spate irrigation;

(e) Institutionalizing poverty alleviation strategies, including increased access to credit in rural areas.

Although some of these measures had positive effects on poverty and water supply, the water and drought-related problems of Yemen have outpaced the Government's ability to mitigate their effects. Many agricultural and poverty alleviation policies of the past, such as low-interest loans, subsidized diesel pricing, unpriced or below-cost priced water, uncontrolled groundwater drilling, banning the import of fruits and vegetables, and public investment in surface or spate irrigation, have effectively encouraged the further depletion of groundwater. Although many of these policies have since been reversed, the Government largely lacks the technical means, legal instruments, and political will to regulate groundwater extraction. Yemen's fragmented geography and hydrology and the predominance of the dispersed rural population make centralized control difficult. Most of the population and economic activity are concentrated in the water-depleted western highlands, making it difficult to explore alternative sources of supply such as desalination.

---

[240] World Bank, "Country Brief: Middle East & North Africa Region - Yemen".

[241] Ibid.

[242] ESCWA, *Review and Appraisal of Progress Made by Yemen in the Implementation of the New Programme of Action for the Least Developed Countries for the 1990s*, p. 29.

[243] Interview with Naji Abu Hatim, Senior Rural Development Specialist, Department of Rural Development, Water & Environment, World Bank, Sana'a, Yemen, 7 March 2005.

Nevertheless, the Government has recognized the need to take measures to avert a drought or water-related disaster. However, Government response to drought has been reactionary, as no early warning system or national drought preparedness plan has been established. In 2005, the Government developed a national water strategy within the National Water Resources Authority (NWRA), which will give national water resource management much needed focus. However, the extreme socio-economic vulnerability of Yemen to drought emphasizes the necessity of developing strategies to mitigate future drought occurrences, beyond water resources management. The Government remains committed to addressing the issues of poverty and food insecurity, which are strongly linked to water shortage and drought. In 2003, Yemen became the first country in the ESCWA region to administer a Food Insecurity and Vulnerability Information and Mapping System (FIVIMS) survey, with FAO assistance.[244] The survey identifies food insecurities, their locations, coping mechanisms and consumption habits, and intra-household impacts. Because the issues of food insecurity and socio-economic drought are strongly linked in Yemen, this initiative serves as a base for monitoring socio-economic drought and preparing a national socio-economic drought preparedness plan. Although the survey and national water strategy are first steps towards drought preparedness, Yemen still faces challenges in establishing a drought preparedness plan.

1. *Institutional capacity*

A significant obstacle to integrated water resources management and drought preparedness in Yemen was the absence of a central water authority and a national water policy. In 1995, the Government consolidated the water resources management functions under a single authority, NWRA, and put in place a legislative framework to support its functions. Currently, other institutions involved in water supply, management and use are the Ministry of Agriculture and Irrigation, Ministry of Water and Environment, the Agriculture Research and Extension Authority (AREA), and NWSA. The NWRA monitors the supply of water within the country, regularly producing data on water supply and quality. Based on eight well-distributed stations in the three agro-ecological zones, AREA conducts agricultural research and monitors plant and animal life in Yemen. Within AREA there is also a Resource Management Centre, which works to map land use, cover and degradation.[245]

Despite the progress in establishing central water and agricultural management organizations, institutional arrangements for central drought monitoring and drought early warning are lacking in Yemen. Drought monitoring is not conducted, but rather attention is focused on issues of water supply expansion, crop yield improvement, and self-sufficiency in vegetable and fruit production. Agriculture and water management institutions are relatively young, and institutional capacity and authority are still weak. Water demand management has, for the most part, not been instituted in Yemen, and irrigation water is provided free of cost. For example, 100,000 individual well owners take groundwater management decisions without Government regulation. Integrated water resources management remains a challenge, particularly as water demand has already outpaced supply in some parts of Yemen. Therefore, significant changes in the institutional structures and water resources policies would be necessary to enable a more multidisciplinary and integrated approach to drought preparedness.

2. *Technical capacity and monitoring*

Data on Yemen are scant and not always comprehensive or reliable, which constitutes a significant obstacle to drought monitoring.[246] Furthermore, available data are rarely shared between academic, research and government institutions, nor are they shared among government institutions. Information exchange is not a policy and generally only occurs at the individual level. Moreover, in all these institutions, there is a

---

[244] Interview with Ibrahim, Thabet, Program Director, FAO - Yemen, Sana'a, Yemen, March 7, 2005.

[245] Interview with Isma'il Muharram, Chairman of Agriculture Research and Extension Authority, Ministry of Agriculture, Sana'a, Yemen, 7 March 2005.

[246] Interview with Abdulkader Ali, Project Director for Geo-Environmental Information Project, Advisory Services on the Development and Use of Geo-Environmental Information Integrated Water Resources Management, Sana'a, Yemen, 7 March 2005.

shortage of trained scientists, owing in part to brain drain emigration.[247] In general, there is also a lack of analytical tools for drought monitoring, and a lack of harmonized information products.[248] GIS capacity is limited in Yemen, but growing. Within the AREA Resource Management Centre, there is a GIS database, operating at strong technical capacity with the potential to generate drought data. However, no baseline study has been carried out on drought, and the current information on drought is ad hoc and without a focal institution.

---

[247] Interview with Isma'il Muharram, Chairman of Agriculture Research and Extension Authority, Ministry of Agriculture, Sana'a, Yemen, 7 March 2005.

[248] I. Muharram, S. Nahdi and A.M. Bamatraf, "The National Agricultural Research System of Yemen", WANA NARS Study (1999) – Yemen (Aleppo, ICARDA, 1999).

VIII. PREVENTING AND MITIGATING SOCIO-ECONOMIC DROUGHT IN THE ESCWA REGION: SUMMARY AND CONCLUSIONS

The 1999-2000 drought, the worst in decades in the ESCWA region, resulted in enhanced awareness of the need for greater drought mitigation and preparedness measures. To that end, many Governments in the region have taken steps towards developing drought preparedness capacity nationally; examples include Jordan's plan to develop a drought unit within the NCARTT and Yemen's food security survey. Many countries have also worked to enhance their GIS technical capacity for drought monitoring and other purposes. Recent efforts have led to the establishment of new regional drought networks, such as the ICARDA NEMEDCA. The Network services all the ESCWA members: Egypt (the Nile Valley and the Red Sea), Iraq, Jordan, Lebanon, Palestine, Syrian Arab Republic, Bahrain, Kuwait, Oman, Qatar, Saudi Arabia, United Arab Emirates and Yemen.

Despite the above measures, there is still not an expanded awareness of drought and its impacts, as well as a capacity to mitigate it, in the ESCWA region. Although some countries possess well-equipped meteorological networks and systems, a lack of adequate drought monitoring institutions, tools, and information production and sharing on a region-wide basis has severely limited national capacities to predict and prepare for drought. Owing to the complexities of drought disasters, however, the study of drought has largely focused on limited-area case-studies, often within national boundaries. Such studies on drought within the ESCWA region have generally been ad hoc, and lack perspective on what constitutes a socio-economic drought, on how drought disasters can be mitigated, and on the general applicability of early warning systems, particularly for the region as a whole. In the 1999-2000 drought, a large section of the ESCWA region was affected, each country differently, in large part owing to disparities in societal vulnerability to drought. Regional drought research should therefore examine the ways in which non-climatic factors affect societal vulnerability to drought, and which drought planning and mitigation approaches can help to reduce this vulnerability. The following section outlines efforts to be undertaken to prevent and mitigate socio-economic drought in the region.

A. BUILD INSTITUTIONAL AND TECHNICAL CAPACITY

1. *National drought monitoring institutions*

National-level drought preparedness plans and early warning systems are virtually non-existent in the ESCWA region. Moreover, the region lacks central institutions or task forces charged with assessing drought and developing a drought preparedness plan. There is also a need for the development of long-term drought planning, rather than the crisis management approach of the past in which drought mitigation committees are set up once drought is apparent, and disbanded once the drought subsides. The three main functions of drought planning are: (a) monitoring and early warning; (b) risk assessment; and (c) response and mitigation. Accordingly, there is a need for each ESCWA member to establish a central national coordinating body or authority, charged with assessing drought risk, developing drought planning and preparedness methodologies and strategies, disseminating the drought risk findings, educating policy makers on the importance of improved drought preparedness as part of integrated water resources management, and developing a drought early warning system. This body, housed in a coordinating Ministry, would continually compile, interpret and report on all relevant data sources to monitor drought extent and impact.[249]

2. *Multidisciplinary linkages*

A socio-economic drought early warning system operates through a multidisciplinary approach. Institutional arrangements and inter-agency communication and information exchange are therefore crucial to its success. An adjustment of decision-making to accord priority to integrating information, policy and planning is necessary for the establishment of a drought preparedness plan and early warning system. Gradual but significant changes in the institutional structures of governments would be necessary to enable a more multidisciplinary and integrated approach to decision-making, especially in drought-vulnerable

---

[249] E. DePauw, "Drought Early Warning Systems in West Asia and North Africa".

economic sectors and communities. Partnerships between disciplines and institutions will further strengthen cooperation and enhance transparency. Important issues to be addressed are the institutional linkages between monitoring and rapid response action at different decision-making levels.[250]

3. *Meteorological and hydrological capacity-building*

There is also a need to enhance the institutional capacity of national meteorological and hydrological services to assess drought and produce and disseminate regular and reliable data. Specifically, there is a need to (a) support and strengthen systems for the systematic collection and processing of meteorological hydrological data; (b) build and strengthen scientific networks for the enhancement of scientific and technical capacities of meteorological, hydrological, agricultural and socio-economic professionals dealing with drought; (c) develop inventories of climate and water resources indicators and indices; (d) enhance the understanding of socio-economic drought and drought phenomena and of the causes of drought; and (e) develop decision support models for analysis of drought data.

4. *Information exchange*

Drought information exchange in the ESCWA region should be institutionalized and greatly enhanced since it often occurs on ad hoc basis and not as a matter of policy. Drought early warning would benefit greatly from enhanced collaboration between responsible ministries and institutions within a country, as well as within the region.[251] Insufficient communication and collaboration between relevant drought-monitoring and disaster-planning bodies hinder the timely flow of information essential to early warning and vulnerability assessments. Easy and unlimited access to data is crucial to effective early warning;[252] it could be enhanced by the use of the web to facilitate information delivery for both national and regional information exchange.

5. *Regional network*

The ICARDA NEMEDCA, and other regional networks, can be used as examples to build on in meeting a crucial need. There must be support for regional drought networks and information exchange to streamline the flow of information on monitoring tools and technologies, on assessment methodologies and early warning data. Networks also serve to build national capacity by promoting professional contacts, study tours, expert group meetings and training courses.[253] Thus networking provides opportunities to share experiences and lessons learned. In addition, networks can serve as focal points for regional drought monitoring, vulnerability assessment, and early warning, thereby supporting national drought-monitoring institutions.[254]

B. HARMONIZE AND MONITOR SOCIO-ECONOMIC DROUGHT METHODOLOGIES AND INDICATORS

The development of common reporting standards in data collection remains a challenge for the accurate assessment of drought. Socio-economic behavioural changes and coping mechanisms of communities affected by drought are not currently systematically captured by drought early warning

---

[250] Ibid.

[251] ISDR, *Living with Risk: A Global Review of Disaster Reduction Initiatives* (Geneva, Inter-Agency Secretariat of the United Nations International Strategy for Disaster Reduction, 2004).

[252] United Nations Convention to Combat Desertification, "Early Warning Systems: report of the ad hoc Panel" (ICCD/COP(4)/CST/4), Conference of the Parties, Committee on Science and Technology, fourth session, Bonn, December 2000.

[253] ICARDA, "International network to help countries cope with drought", ICARDA *Caravan* 17 (Aleppo, December 2002).

[254] IUCN Centre for Mediterranean Cooperation and Global Water Partnership - Mediterranean, "Drought Preparedness and Risk Management in the Mediterranean Region", paper presented by T.A. El Hassani at Water, Wetlands and Climate Change: Building Linkages for their Integrated Management, Mediterranean Regional Roundtable held in Athens in 2002 (Gland, Switzerland, International Union for the Conservation of Nature, 2002).

systems, nor have these systems incorporated methods for capturing the economic losses associated with drought.[255] Therefore, challenges remain in the ESCWA region, and worldwide, with regard to the effective incorporation of the socio-economic dimensions of drought according to internationally developed and accepted standards.

1. *Indicators*

A critical component in planning for drought is the provision of timely and reliable meteorological, environmental, economic and social information. This information, if applied in a timely and effective manner, can help to reduce the impact of drought through the establishment of a drought early warning system. Different indicators and information sources are needed to assess various characteristics of drought, such as intensity, exceptionality, impact, and spatial extent of each dimension. Meteorological data and analytical tools to transform drought-monitoring data into relevant drought indicators are critical for the adequate monitoring of drought and drought vulnerability assessment, as demonstrated by international best practices. Since there is a general lack of analytical tools for drought monitoring, and of suitable information products in the ESCWA region, the meteorological services should build on well-established drought indicators.[256] Incorporation of socio-economic data that accurately serve as predictors of socio-economic drought is crucial in predicting and mitigating its effects. Socio-economic indicators and indices should be developed based on country-specific vulnerabilities benefiting from international standards and should be applied to ensure harmonization of national and cross-country drought analysis.

2. *Data collection and delivery*

The ESCWA region does not have a historical drought database, which is essential for determining drought patterns in the region.[257] Therefore, drought data are in large part not reliable, harmonized or standardized, and are, for the most part, not timely. Data sharing networks are weak, with inadequate density and quality of meteorological and hydrological data,[258] while water and climate data sharing networks are ineffectual or non-existent at both the national and regional levels.[259] The capacity for reliable data generation and effective and responsive data delivery systems needs improvement in the region.

3. *Drought assessment*

Early warning systems should examine the full range of biological, climatic, agricultural, environmental, social and economic factors involved in drought. Drought vulnerability assessments must incorporate influences on drought on regions, populations, livelihoods, socio-economic activities, and the like, taking into account the range of prevailing coping strategies of the population at risk and the capacity of the government to provide mitigating assistance. Drought vulnerability assessments should also build on existing hazard risk methodologies and vulnerability analysis toolkits for emergency planners and policy makers.[260] These toolkits, methodologies and models help to assess the potential impacts of drought. A current, region-specific and prioritized drought impact analysis will reveal sectors, populations, or activities that are most vulnerable to drought and that, when evaluated with the probability of drought occurrence, can identify drought vulnerability.

---

[255] United Nations Convention to Combat Desertification, "Early Warning Systems: report of the ad hoc Panel".

[256] E. DePauw, "Drought early warning systems in West Asia and North Africa".

[257] IUCN, Centre for Mediterranean Cooperation and Global Water Partnership - Mediterranean, "Drought Preparedness and Risk Management in the Mediterranean Region", paper presented by T.A. El Hassani at Water, Wetlands and Climate Change: Building Linkages for their Integrated Management – Mediterranean Regional Roundtable, 2002.

[258] Ibid.

[259] Ibid.

[260] Examples include the Provincial Emergency Program of British Columbia, the Canada Hazard Risk and Vulnerability Analysis Tool Kit, and the United States National Oceanic and Atmospheric Administration community vulnerability assessment step-by-step guide.

4. *Geographic information systems*

A key dimension of drought risk impact assessments is the presentation of the results. An effective tool in increasing understanding and awareness of drought risk and vulnerability impact assessments is hazard mapping, which highlights geographic areas, economic sectors and populations at risk. Geographical information systems are particularly suited for drought monitoring, given their ability to link every item of information to a given location. Remote sensing for the monitoring and mapping of drought is another potentially important research area. Meteorological and other satellite systems can generate, at global and regional scales, a range of indicators related to vegetation health. These are already used in several early warning systems to forecast crop condition and estimate agricultural production.[261]

C. MONITOR DROUGHT AND CONDUCT REGIONAL VULNERABILITY ASSESSMENTS

Regular drought monitoring and drought risk and vulnerability analysis are the key to effective early warning and to the development of drought mitigation policies, since they can help identify pockets of vulnerability at the regional level.

1. *Monitoring*

Once drought indicators have been established and standardized, routine monitoring of the hydrologic cycle, vulnerable communities and socio-economic activities, is the basis for objective recognition of socio-economic drought and preparing to deal with its impacts. Currently, drought monitoring in the ESCWA region is neither standardized nor regular, and information generated therein is not always shared. Most meteorological and hydrological services in ESCWA member countries track precipitation departures from average, other climatic variables, stream flow, groundwater and reservoir levels, and soil moisture. This is an important first step. While vegetation conditions are often monitored using satellite-derived data, where available in the region, monitoring socio-economic indicators provides a more comprehensive perspective of the potential impacts of drought. The ability to monitor and disseminate critical drought-related information has been enhanced by new technologies such as automated weather stations, satellites, computers, and improved communication techniques.[262] Such technological advances should be employed to ensure regular monitoring of drought indicators for their timely incorporation in drought vulnerability assessments.

2. *Vulnerability assessment*

Vulnerability assessment is a key component of early warning, making it possible to identify vulnerable areas, communities and activities so that action can be taken to mitigate the effects of drought. Drought vulnerability assessments, examining the consequences of a drought and society's resilience or vulnerability to it, must reflect any changes in social, economic and environmental conditions. Since drought impacts extend beyond the area physically affected by drought and can linger after the event has ended, drought vulnerability assessments must be conducted regularly to ensure that dissemination of drought risk findings to key policy and decision-makers remains accurate and up-to-date for effective drought mitigation.

Region-wide, there is a need to establish institutional capacity to assess the frequency, severity, and localization of droughts, their potential impacts on the agricultural sector, the environment, and the livelihoods and well-being of the affected populations. On that basis, vulnerability profiles can be assessed and drought-vulnerable activities, sectors, populations, and sub-regions can be determined and targeted.[263]

---

[261] E. DePauw, "Drought in WANA: six frequently asked questions", ICARDA *Caravan* 17, December 2002.

[262] American Meteorological Society, "AMS policy statement on meteorological drought", 1996.

[263] IUCN Centre for Mediterranean Cooperation and Global Water Partnership - Mediterranean, "Drought Preparedness and Risk Management in the Mediterranean Region", paper presented by T.A. El Hassani at Water, Wetlands and Climate Change: Building Linkages for their Integrated Management-Mediterranean Regional Roundtable, 2002.

D. CREATE DROUGHT PREPAREDNESS STRATEGIES AND EARLY WARNING SYSTEMS

The 1999-2001 drought and its profound socio-economic impacts have confirmed the need for national drought preparedness strategies. Currently, no ESCWA member State has a drought preparedness plan. Timely information and early warning are the foundation of effective drought preparedness plans.

1. *National drought strategies*

There is an increasingly urgent need for the ESCWA member States to draft national plans of action and regional strategies for drought mitigation, making clear the role of central and provincial ministries, agencies, non-governmental organizations (NGOs) and communities in implementing drought response programmes. National plans would allow for strengthening institutional arrangements, planning for drought, and developing policy-making mechanisms for drought mitigation. National drought mitigation strategies allow for the integration of policy planning in socio-economic and natural resource fields.[264] A drought strategy will shed light on detrimental policies and allow for improved policy planning, and should therefore include sufficient capacity for contingency planning before the onset of drought and for appropriate policies to reduce vulnerability and increase resilience to drought. Collaboration with and participation from concerned ministries are crucial to a successful strategy. Policies that promote the development and implementation of regionally appropriate drought mitigation measures will help to reduce the future costs of drought, whether or not future changes in climate alter the frequency and intensity of meteorological drought.[265]

2. *Early warning*

A national strategy depends heavily on data sharing, early warning system products, drought forecasts, drought monitoring tools, vulnerability assessment methodologies, integrated drought monitoring, and delivery systems.[266] Drought plans should include the development of an integrated climate monitoring and delivery system for distributing information to decision makers in a timely manner. Such a plan also should include development of a drought monitoring system, based largely on meteorological, climatic, hydrologic and socio-economic information. An effective monitoring system will aid in the development of improved drought assessment methodologies by providing early warning of drought impacts, as well as a context for planning for drought events against the backdrop of longer-term climate trends and variations.[267] Dissemination of early warning findings to key policy and decision-makers is critical to effective drought preparedness, and users should be trained in the application of this information to decision-making.

E. REDUCE VULNERABILITY THROUGH INTEGRATED POLICY PLANNING

1. *Policy integration*

Since drought mitigation is multidisciplinary by nature, strategies should be integrated into national policies affecting water supply, water use, land use, and environmental and agricultural policies. In the ESCWA region, decision-making systems separate economic, technological, social, and environmental factors at the policy, planning and management levels. An adjustment of decision-making to enable a more multidisciplinary and integrated approach to decision-making and to integrate drought planning is necessary to reduce vulnerability to drought. Education and awareness of drought, potential drought impacts, and drought assessment and delivery tools for key policy makers are important to achieving a cohesive drought strategy, and to integrating national natural resource, agricultural and environmental policies.[268] Drought

---

[264] Ibid.

[265] American Meteorological Society, "AMS policy statement on meteorological drought", 1996.

[266] ISDR, *Living with Risk: A Global Review of Disaster Reduction Initiatives* (Geneva, Inter-Agency Secretariat of the United Nations International Strategy for Disaster Reduction, 2004).

[267] American Meteorological Society, "AMS policy statement on meteorological drought", 1996.

[268] Ibid.

management strategies should include sufficient capacity for contingency planning before the onset of drought and appropriate policies to reduce vulnerability and increase resilience to it.

2. *Land use and agriculture*

When demands on land and water resources exceed their sustainable levels, land degradation and desertification become an increasingly limiting factor, decreasing the land's productivity. In the ESCWA region, agricultural stresses on the natural resources of the region have exceeded the carrying capacity in many countries, which is evidenced by the increasing rate of desertification and the region's vulnerability to drought. The most effective buffer against drought is the application of proven dry land management principles and improved land use patterns. This would translate, for example, into refraining from growing crops in marginal environments, reducing water consumption, and grazing rangelands according to their carrying capacity.[269] In rain-fed semi-arid conditions, the goal of soil fertility and agronomic management is to optimize the efficient use of water and thus mitigate the effects of drought. Fertilization, apart from increasing crop yield, also ensures higher water-use efficiency. Policies to halt land degradation and improve soil productivity (such as leaving lands fallow to recover in times of drought), terracing, and reforestation are essential components of drought mitigation. Policies that encourage over-exploitation of water, such as diesel subsidies for water pumps, un-priced or under-priced irrigation water, and subsidies for water-intensive agricultural production, should be terminated. Instead, policies that help to reduce land degradation and buffer agricultural communities against drought should be promoted, including increased access to credit, development of reserve stocks of grain, and agricultural insurance.

3. *Integrated water resources management*

Management of scarce water resources lies at the heart of drought preparedness and mitigation. While there have been water-related drought-mitigating developments, such as increased crop yields with increased irrigation, progress in cloud-seeding technologies, and discoveries of underground aquifers, the grim reality is that water availability in the ESCWA region is not likely to increase in the future. Given that ground and surface waters have exceeded their sustainable capacities in many countries, agriculture will have to share a static or diminishing water supply, strained by ever-growing urban, industrial and recreational demand. Thus, the only viable alternative is to cope with drought, and to come to terms with the reality of limited water supplies and rising human needs. The key to drought mitigation is improved integrated water resources management. Effective IWRM must include (a) policies to improve water-use efficiency, particularly in irrigation; (b) education of policy makers on the importance of improved drought preparedness as part of IWRM; (c) pricing water according to its economic costs; (d) rationing water if necessary; and (e) developing non-traditional water sources such as water reuse, water harvesting, fog harvesting, and desalinization.[270]

---

[269] ICARDA, "Plant nutrition and agronomic practices: prerequisites for drought mitigation", ICARDA *Caravan* 17, (Aleppo, December 2002).

[270] ISDR. *Living with Risk: A Global Review of Disaster Reduction Initiatives* (Geneva, Inter-Agency Secretariat of the United Nations International Strategy for Disaster Reduction, 2004).

Annex I

QUESTIONNAIRE PREPARED FOR COUNTRY STUDIES

Country's vulnerability to drought

Which areas of the country are particularly vulnerable to drought? Why? (Do you have a drought map – rainfall distribution, agro-ecological zones, land use mapping, and rain-fed vs. irrigated farming?)

Which populations are most affected by drought in the country?

- What is their primary economic activity? (livestock, settled farmers, type of farming, irrigated/rain-fed farming, nomadic, poor urban, landless, small-land holder, villages)

- What are their sources of income? (multiple sources, rain-dependent?) How are their sources of income impacted by drought?

- Do government services access them? (statistics such as access to water/sanitation)

- How are they impacted during drought? (loss of livelihood, loss of assets, migration)

- What are their coping mechanisms? (such as borrowing, finding off-farm work, decreasing food intake, selling off livestock) Do coping mechanisms differ by age group and gender? (Do children, the elderly and women feel the impact of drought first and hardest?)

- Are human behaviours worsening the impacts of drought in the country? How? (land degradation patterns based on land and water uses)

Environmental impact

What have been the general environmental impacts of drought in country?

- Increased desertification? Any data supporting?

- Has drought impacted biodiversity? How? Supporting data?

- Has drought threatened any specific animal or plant species? Which ones? Could these be indicator of plant or animal species for an early warning system?

Has drought caused the loss or destruction of any ecosystems? Which ones?

Government response

In the 1999-2001 drought or other recent droughts, what was the Government response?

- Who was assisted and how?

- Was there any international intervention? Describe.

- Was there any Government early warning or information dissemination on the drought, or actions to be taken (such as hygiene measures, water conservation methods, water catchment)? In what form? From which institution?

Drought monitoring institutional capacity

Describe the Drought Monitoring System in the country.

- Which institutions are involved?

- What kind of data is collected? Any socio-economic data?

- What exactly is monitored? (precipitation, climate, crops, food security)
- Which institution is responsible for drought information dissemination? Drought data collection?

Is there a national drought preparedness plan in the country?

- Which institution is responsible? What is their authority (reporting to prime ministry)?
- How are drought vulnerability assessments made?
- Are these assessments/forecasts accurate?
- Who receives information about impending droughts?

What is the technical capacity of the drought monitoring system?

- What is lacking?
- Training, equipment, institutional capacity?

What is the status of information-sharing among agricultural, meteorological and other drought-monitoring institutions?

- Is information shared? At a price? (Are meteorological data easily accessible for free?)
- Is information easily exchanged among academics, agricultural research, farming communities and drought monitoring institutions?
- Is there a central body that collects information related to drought? Could this body act as a drought early warning data collection and processing centre?

What is needed to achieve a socio-economic drought early warning system (a drought early warning system that also monitors the socio-economic impacts of drought)?

- Challenges?
- Constraints? (financial, technical, institutional)

WILHITE DROUGHT PLANNING METHODOLOGY

10 Steps for Drought Planning

1. Appoint a Drought Task Force
2. State the Purpose and Objectives of the Drought Plan
3. Seek Stakeholder Participation and Resolve Conflict
4. Inventory Resources and Identify Groups at Risk
5. Develop Organizational Structure and Prepare Drought Plan
6. Integrate Science and Policy, Close Institutional Gaps
7. Publicize the Proposed Plan, Solicit Reaction
8. Implement the Plan
9. Develop Education Programs
10. Conduct Post-Drought Evaluation

For information on the Wilhite drought planning methodology, refer to
http://www.drought.unl.edu/plan/handbook/process.htm

Annex III

SOCIO-ECONOMIC DROUGHT EARLY WARNING SYSTEM:
SAMPLE INDICATORS

Water resource indicators	Environment indicators
Actual renewable water resources: per capita	Ecosystem area
Agricultural water use intensity	Deforestation rate
Desalination: desalinated water production	Desertification rate
Ecosystem area: water bodies	Land use, arable (%)
Freshwater indices: water poverty index	Biodiversity
Groundwater withdrawals: per capita annual average	Abundance of wildlife
Groundwater withdrawals: percentage used for agricultural purposes	Vegetation cover
Groundwater withdrawals: withdrawals as a percentage of annual recharge	Incidence of dust storms
Industrial water pollution: organic pollutant emissions (BOD)	Evaporation rates
Internal renewable water resources (IRWR): Dependency ratio	Soil infiltration rates
Internal renewable water resources (IRWR): per capita annual average	Trade in forest products: exports, value
Internal renewable water resources: groundwater recharge per capita	
Internal renewable water resources: surface water produced internally	
River flows: annual river flows from other countries	
River flows: annual river flows to other countries	
Species: fish species, number	
Water withdrawals: annual total	
Water withdrawals: as a percentage of internal water resources	
Water withdrawals: per capita annual total	
Water withdrawals: percentage used for agricultural purposes	
Demographic indicators	**Health/nutrition indicators**
Population growth rate	Immunization rates against water-borne diseases
Rural-urban migration	Death rates for water borne-diseases
Refugees: internally displaced peoples, number assisted by United Nations High Commissioner for Refugees (UNHCR)	Children's health: infant mortality rate
Refugees: internally displaced peoples, total number	Children's health: mortality rate in children under 5
Population: growth rate of total population	Children's health: oral rehydration therapy (ORT) use rate
Population: population density	Children's health: underweight children under 5-- moderate and severe
Urban and rural areas: growth rate of rural population	Children's health: wasting in children under 5-- moderate and severe
Urban and rural areas: growth rate of urban population	Reduction of food consumption by gender, age group
Urban and rural areas: rural population	Physicians per 1,000 population
Urban and rural areas: urban population	Female literacy
Urban and rural areas: urban population as a percentage of total population	Nutrition: calorie supply per capita
Demographics: total fertility rate	Public health: annual per capita health expenditure
Education: average length of schooling, female	Public health: physicians per 100,000 people
Population above 65 years	Public health: public health expenditures as % of total

Economic indicators	Access indicators
GDP: percentage from industry	Access to information: digital access index
GDP: percentage from agriculture	Transportation: total road network
GDP: percentage from manufacturing	Access to information: cellular mobile telephone subscribers
GDP: percentage from services	Access to information: Internet hosts, number
Income equality: Gini Index	Access to information: Internet users, number
Income equality: share of total income, all quintiles	Access to information: radios per 1,000 people
Poverty: national poverty rates	Access to information: television sets per 1,000 people
Poverty: population living on less than $1/day; $2/day	
Poverty gap US$/day , US$2/day	
Trade in agriculture: food imports as a percentage of total merchandise imports	
Debt: present value of debt as a percentage of gross national income (GNI)	
Debt: total debt service	
Debt: total external debt	
Development assistance: assistance per capita	
Development assistance: assistance, percentage of GNI	
Development assistance: assistance, percentage of government expenditures	
Trade in agriculture: agricultural raw materials as a percentage of total merchandise exports	
Trade in agriculture: agricultural raw materials as a percentage of total merchandise imports	
Trade in agriculture: food exports as a percentage of total merchandise exports	
Trade in agriculture: food imports as a percentage of total merchandise imports	

BIBLIOGRAPHY

Alabsi, A.A. 2001. Country Pasture/Forage Resource Profiles: Yemen. Rome, Food and Agriculture Organization of the United Nations, November 2001.

Al-Qadhi, M.H. 2003. Thirst for water and development leads to conflict in Yemen. *Choices, The Human Development Magazine.* New York, UNDP, March 2003. http://www.undp.org/dpa/choices/2003/march/yemen.html.

Althawr, A. 1999. Contribution to the Agriculture Sector Review in Yemen. Ministry of Agriculture and Irrigation, Yemen, February 1999.

American Meteorological Society. 1996. AMS policy statement on meteorological drought. http://www.ametsoc.org/policy/drought.html.

Aw-Hassan, A., Alsanabani, M., and A.R. Bamatraf. 1999. Step forward, Yemen terraces. ICARDA *Caravan 10.* Aleppo, Syrian Arab Republic.

Carter and others. 1988. Agriculture. In Syria: A Country Study. Country Study Series, U.S. Government Printing Office, 1988. http://www.country-studies.com/.

CLIMAS. 2004. Drought planning and mitigation: social vulnerability. University of Arizona, Climate Assessment for the Southwest, The Institute for the Study of Planet Earth. http://www.ispe.arizona.edu/climas/research/drought/social.html.

DePauw, E. 2004. Drought early warning systems in West Asia and North Africa. Aleppo, Syrian Arab Republic, International Center for Agricultural Research in the Dry Areas (ICARDA).

————. 2002. Drought in WANA: six frequently asked questions. ICARDA *Caravan* 17, December 2002.

————. 2001. An Agro-ecological Exploration of the Arabian Peninsula. Aleppo, Syrian Arab Republic, ICARDA, December 2001.

De Sherbinin, A., and V. Dompka, eds. 1998. *Water and Population Dynamics: Case Studies and Policy Implications,* Case study: Jordan, population dynamics in arid regions: the experience of the Azraq Oasis conservation project by F. Fariz and A. Hatough-Bouran. American Association for the Advancement of Science. http://www.aaas.org/international/ehn/waterpop/jordan.htm.

Economic and Social Commission for Western Asia (ESCWA), Federal Institute for Geosciences and Natural Resources, Germany (BGR), and Deutsche Gesellschaft für Technische Zusammenarbeit (GTZ) GmbH. 2004. *Enhancing Negotiation Skills on International Water Issues in the ESCWA Region.* Beirut, 2004.

ESCWA. 2004. Where do Arab Women Stand in the Development Process? A Gender-Based Statistical Analysis.

————. 2002. Survey of Economic and Social Developments in the ESCWA Region, 2001-2002 (E/ESCWA/ED/2002/8).

————. 2001. Review and Appraisal of Progress Made by Yemen in the Implementation of the New Programme of Action for the Least Developed Countries for the 1990s (E/ESCWA/ED/2001/17).

————. 2000. Application of Sustainable Development Indicators in the ESCWA Member Countries: Analysis of Results (E/ESCWA/ED/2000/4).

————. 1999. Updating the Assessment of Water Resources in the ESCWA Member Countries. Beirut, October 1999.

————. 1997. Regional Report: Implementation of Agenda 21: Review of Progress Made since the United Nations Conference on Environment and Development, 1992. Beirut, April 1997. http://www.un.org/esa/earthsummit/ecwa-cp.htm#chap11.

Earth Observatory. 2005. Drought: The Creeping Disaster. Florida, NASA. http://earthobservatory.nasa.gov/Library/DroughtFacts/.

FAO. 2004. FAOSTAT Online Database. Rome, Food and Agriculture Organization of the United Nations. http://faostat.fao.org.

————. 2004. AQUASTAT Online Database. Rome, Food and Agriculture Organization of the United Nations. http://www.fao.org.

————. 2004. TerraStat Online Database. Rome, Food and Agriculture Organization of the United Nations. http://www.fao.org.

————. 2002. Yemen national report. Rome, Food and Agriculture Organization of the United Nations, 6 June 2002. http://www.fao.org/ag/agl/swlwpnr/reports/y_nr/z_ye/ye.htm.

————. 2001. Country Pasture/Forage Resource Profiles: Jordan. Rome, Food and Agriculture Organization of the United Nations. http://www.fao.org/WAICENT/faoinfo/economic/giews/english/alertes/1999/SRJOR996.htm#P43_5036.

————. 2001. Country Pasture/Forage Resource Profiles: Syria. Rome, Food and Agriculture Organization of the United Nations.

————. 1999. Drought conditions threaten food security of Syria's nomadic livestock producers. Global Watch, Food and Agriculture Organization of the United Nations. Rome, 8 September 1999.

————. 1999. Special Report: FAO/WFP Crop and Food Supply Assessment Mission to the Syrian Arab Republic. Rome, Food and Agriculture Organization of the United Nations, 23 August 1999.

————. 1999. Drought in the Near East: cereal and livestock production down sharply. Global Watch, FAO, Rome, 29 July 1999.

————. 1999. Special Report: Drought Causes Extensive Crop Damage in the Near East, Raising Concerns for Food Supply Difficulty in Some Parts. Rome, 16 July 1999.

————. 1999, Worst drought in decades decimates cereal crops in Jordan. Global Watch, Food and Agriculture Organization of the United Nations. Rome, 3 June 1999.

————. 1999. Adverse effects of drought on domestic food production during 1998/1999 in Iraq. Baghdad, Food and Agriculture Organization of the United Nations in Iraq, May 1999.

————. 1999. FAO/WFP Crop and Food Supply Assessment Mission to the Kingdom of Jordan. Rome, Food and Agriculture Organization of the United Nations, 26 May 1999.

FAO and the World Bank. 2001. Farming Systems and Poverty: Improving Farmers' Livelihoods in a Changing World.

Hayes, M. 2005. What is drought? Drought indices. National Drought Mitigation Center, University of Nebraska-Lincoln, 2005. http://www.drought.unl.edu/whatis/what.htm.

Hazell, P., Oram, P., and N. Chaherli. 2001. Managing droughts in the low-rainfall areas of the Middle East and North Africa. Washington, D.C., International Food Policy Research Institute, September 2001.

Huss-Ashmore, R. 1997. Local-level data for use as early warning indicators. Philadelphia, University of Pennsylvania. Internet Journal of African Studies, vol.2, March 1997. http://www.bradford.ac.uk/research/ijas/ijasno2/ashmore.html.

International Center for Agricultural Research in the Dry Areas (ICARDA). 2004. Poverty, Food Systems and Nutritional Well-Being of Children in North West Syria. ICARDA Development Seminar Series. Aleppo, Syrian Arab Republic.

————. 2002. International network to help countries cope with drought. ICARDA *Caravan* 17, Aleppo, December 2002.

————. 1998. The West Asian Joint Program for Drought Preparedness and Mitigation of the Effects of Drought, Sub-Regional Program on Combating Desertification and Drought in Western Asia. Aleppo Syrian Arab Republic, November 1998.

————. 1998. Drought preparedness and mitigation of the effects of drought. Paper presented at the Expert Group Meeting for the Preparation of the Sub-Regional Action Program on Combating Desertification and Drought in Western Asia. Muscat, Oman, September 1998.

ILO. 2004. Global Employment Trends. Geneva, International Labour Organization. http://www.ilo.org/public/english/employment/strat/download/trends.pdf.

Interview with Abdel Nabi Fardous, Director General, National Center for Agricultural Research and Technology Transfer, Amman, Jordan, 22 March 2005.

Interview with Safa' Mazaher, GIS Lab Administrator, National Center for Agricultural Research and Technology Transfer, Amman, Jordan, 22 March 2005.

Interview with Fayez Bataineh, Ministry of Water and Irrigation, Amman, Jordan, 21 March 2005.

Interview with Abdulkader Ali, Project Director for Geo-Environmental Information Project, Advisory Services on the Development and Use of Geo-Environmental Information Integrated Water Resources Management, Sana'a, Yemen, 7 March 2005.

Interview with Ibrahim Thabet, Director, FAO-Yemen, Sana'a, Yemen, 7 March 2005.

Interview with Isma'il Muharram, Chairman of Agricultural Research and Extension Authority, Sana'a, Yemen, 7 March 2005.

Interview with Naji Abu Hatim, Senior Rural Development Specialist, Department of Rural Development, Water & Environment, World Bank, Sana'a, Yemen, 7 March 2005.

Interview with Jamal Jamaleddin, Director of Training, Research, and International Projects, Ministry of Irrigation, Damascus, Syrian Arab Republic, 28 February 2005.

Interview with Akhtar Ali Rana, Water Resources Engineer. Natural Resource Management Program at ICARDA. Aleppo, 27 February 2005.

IPCC. 2000. *IPCC Special Report on the Regional Impacts of Climate Change: An Assessment of Vulnerability*, chap. 7, Middle East and Arid Asia. Geneva, Intergovernmental Panel on Climate Change. http://www.ipcc.ch.

ISDR. 2004. Drought—Living with Risk: An Integrated Approach to Reducing Societal Vulnerability to Drought. ISDR Ad Hoc Discussion Group on Drought. Geneva, International Strategy for Disaster Reduction. http://www.unisdr.org/eng/about_isdr/bd-lwr-2004-eng.htm.

———. 2004. *Living with Risk: A Global Review of Disaster Reduction Initiatives.* Geneva, Inter-Agency Secretariat of the United Nations International Strategy for Disaster Reduction.

ISDR and WMO. 2004. *Water and disasters: Be informed and be prepared.* Geneva.

IUCN (International Union for the Conservation of Nature and Natural Resources). 2002. Drought Preparedness and Risk Management in the Mediterranean Region. Paper by T.A. El Hassani presented at Water, Wetlands and Climate Change: Building Linkages for their Integrated Management at the Mediterranean Regional Roundtable held at Athens. Gland, Switzerland.

Jordan – vegetation and precipitation. 1978. Jordan Maps, Perry-Castañeda Library Map Collection, University of Texas at Austin, Austin Texas, USA: 1978. http://www.lib.utexas.edu/maps/jordan.html.

Jordan facing water shortage. 1998. US Water News Online, July 1998.

Jordan announces summer water rationing plan for parched kingdom. 2000. Associated Press, 26 April.

Knutson, C., Hayes, M., and T. Philips. 1998. How to Reduce Drought Risk. Western Drought Coordination Council, 1998. http://www.drought.unl.edu/plan/handbook/risk.pdf.

Malakouti, M. 2003. The role of zinc on the yield and grain fortification of wheat in the calcareous soils of dry lands. Paper presented at the Seventh International Conference on Development of Drylands. Tehran, ICARDA, September 2003.

Morris, C. 2000. Drought leads to water row with Turkey. *The Guardian Weekly*, 10 May 2000.

Muharram, I., Nahdi, S., and A.M. Bamatraf. 1999. The National Agricultural Research System of Yemen. WANA NARS Study (1999)-Yemen. Aleppo, ICARDA.

NDMC. 2005. Spotting drought before it's too late. National Drought Mitigation Center, University of Nebraska-Lincoln. http://www.drought.unl.edu/pubs/spotdrt.pdf.

———. 2005. What is drought? National Drought Mitigation Center, University of Nebraska-Lincoln. http://www.drought.unl.edu.

PPEW. 2005. Basics of Early Warning. Platform for the Promotion of Early Warning, Bonn, Germany. http://www.unisdr.org/ppew. http://www.unisdr.org/ppew/whats-ew/basics-ew.htm.

Rinehart., R., and others. 1980. Agriculture. In Jordan: A Country Study. Country Studies Series, U.S. Government Printing Office. http://www.country-studies.com/jordan/agriculture.html.

Rodriguez, A., and others. 1999. Groundwater Use and Supplemental Irrigation in Atareb, Northwest Syria. Aleppo, ICARDA.

Somme, G., and others. 2005. Rainfed Wheat Productivity with Supplemental Irrigation in Al Hasakeh, Northern Syria. Aleppo, ICARDA and the General Commission for Scientific Agricultural Research, Syria.

———. 1999. Micro-catchment Water Harvesting for Improved Vegetative Cover in the Syrian Badia. ICARDA and the General Commission for Scientific Agricultural Research, Syria.

Syria pumps water to Jordan to alleviate drought. 2000. Associated Press, 13 August.

69

United Nations Convention to Combat Desertification. 2000. Early warning systems: report of the ad hoc Panel (ICCD/COP(4)/CST/4). Conference of the Parties, Committee on Science and Technology, fourth session. Bonn, December 2000.

———. 1999. Existing experience of early warning systems and specialized institutions in this field. (ICCD/COP(3)/CST/6). Conference of the Parties, Committee on Science and Technology, third session, Recife, October 1999.

UNDP-DDC. 2005. *Drought Risk and Development Policy.* Discussion paper for the UNDP-DDC/BCPR and UN-ISDR Expert Workshop, 31 January-2-February, 2005. Nairobi. http://www.undp.org/drylands.

UNDP. 2004. Human Development Report Online Database, 2004. http://hdr.undp.org/statistics/data/.

———. 1997. Sustainable Water Resources Management: Programme Outline. UNDP-Yemen, 9 July 1997. http://www.y.net.ye/undp-yem/WTR-OTLN.html.

UNEP. 2004. *Environmental Emergencies News.* Nairobi, United Nations Environment Programme, issue 2, February 2004. http://www.unep.org/DEPI/PDF/Eesnewsletterissue2.pdf.

———. 2002. Disasters: West Asia: Drought. Global Environment Outlook 3. Nairobi, 2002.

———. 1997. Global Environment Outlook –1. Global State of the Environment Report 1997. Nairobi. http://www.unep.org/geo/geo1/ch/ch2_13.htm.

Water shortages plague Jordan. US Water News Online. September 2002. http://www.uswaternews.com/archives/arcglobal/2watsho9.html.

Wilhite, D. A., and M.D. Svoboda. 2000. Drought early warning systems in the context of preparedness and mitigation. Lincoln, Nebraska, National Drought Mitigation Center. http://www.drought.unl.edu/monitor/EWS/ch1_Wilhite.pdf.

Wilson, J. P., and H.J. Bruins. 2005. Food security in the Middle East since 1961. Jacob Blaustein Institute for Desert Research, Ben-Gurion University of the Negev, Sede Boqer, Israel.

World Bank. 2005. Yemen - Rainfed Agriculture and Livestock. Project Information Document. World Bank, Washington, D.C., 1 July.

———. 2005. Water Scarcity in the Middle East and North Africa. Washington, D.C. http://www.worldbank.org.

———. 2005. Country Brief: Middle East & North Africa Region (MENA) – Yemen. Washington, D.C., 2005. http://www.worldbank.org.

———. 2004. World Development Indicators Online Database. Washington, D.C., World Bank. http:///www.worldbank.org/.

———. 2002. Republic of Yemen Poverty Update. Washington, D.C., 11 December 2002.

WHO. 2003. Country Cooperation Strategy for WHO and Syrian Arab Republic: 2003-2007. World Health Organization, Geneva. http://www.who.int/countries/en/cooperation_strategy_syr_en.pdf.

———. 2003. Country Cooperation Strategy for WHO and Jordan, 2003-2007. Cairo, WHO Regional Office for the Eastern Mediterranean. http://www.who.int/countries/en/cooperation_strategy_jor_en.pdf.

WRI. 2004. EarthTrends Online Database. World Resources Institute, Washington, D.C. http://www.wri.org.

———. 2004. Agriculture and Food –Yemen. EarthTrends Country Profiles, EarthTrends Online Database. Washington, D.C., World Resources Institute. http://earthtrends.wri.org/pdf_library/country_profiles/Agr_cou_887.pdf.